Building Bridges in Anthropology:
Understanding, Acting, Teaching,
and Theorizing

Building Bridges in Anthropology: Understanding, Acting, Teaching, and Theorizing

Edited by

Robert Shanafelt

Selected Papers from the Annual Meeting of the
Southern Anthropological Society,
Savannah, Georgia,
February, 2010

Robert Shanafelt, Series Editor

Newfound Press
THE UNIVERSITY OF TENNESSEE LIBRARIES, KNOXVILLE

Southern Anthropological Society

Founded 1966

Building Bridges in Anthropology: Understanding, Acting, Teaching, and Theorizing
© 2012 by Southern Anthropological Society: http://southernanthro.org/

Digital version at www.newfoundpress.utk.edu/pubs/bridges

Newfound Press
University of Tennessee Libraries
1015 Volunteer Boulevard
Knoxville, TN 37996-1000
www.newfoundpress.utk.edu

ISBN-13: 978-0-9846445-3-7
ISBN-10: 0-9846445-3-9

Building bridges in anthropology / edited by Robert Shanafelt ; Robert Shanafelt,
series editor.
Knoxville, Tenn : Newfound Press, University of Tennessee Libraries, c2012.

1 online resource (ix, 242 p.) : ill.
Includes bibliographical references.
1. Ethnology -- History -- 21st century -- Congresses. 2. Anthropology -- History
-- 21st century – Congresses. 3. Ethnology – Southern States -- History -- 21st
century -- Congresses. I. Shanafelt, Robert, 1957-
II. Southern Anthropological Society. Meeting.
GN302.B85 2012

Book design by Jayne W. Rogers
Cover design by Stephanie Thompson

This volume is dedicated to the late Miles Richardson (1932-2011), a dedicated scholar, teacher, and humanitarian who represented the best ideals of anthropological holism.

Contents

PART III Ethnography

Figures

Tables

Photographs

Introduction

Robert Shanafelt

Consider this. If the topics of papers published in anthropology in a given year were jumbled up, smeared together as in an inkblot, like the Rorschach blots of psychological fame, what would we see? Would there emerge in our perception a rather natural-seeming vision of four or five fields? What would the patterns we observe reveal about the nature of our interests? About the field in which we are a part?

Rorschach images are open to interpretation, but that does not mean they lack regularity in response. There are ways of seeing the images that are statistically ordinary and others that are unusual. There is both cultural and individual variation in this patterning. Of course, in anthropology as elsewhere, the way we see things is also only partly constituted by the forms that are given to us. How we see anthropology also reflects historical trajectories of teaching, research work, publications, academic fashions, and our individual dispositions. As self-reflective anthropologists, we might think that we are very sophisticated in understanding this, but it still could be that there are implicit ways we have been taught to see the patterns that lead us to overlook certain other forms that appear obvious to others who have been taught differently.

An inkblot metaphor for our academic discipline is probably too amorphous and vague to capture the nuances of our field and to be of pedagogical use. The more popularly used metaphors are often geographic and geometric. The textbooks commonplace is that of anthropology as a subject with fields, areas, and subdivisions—as if we are describing a plane geometry of farmlands and housing units. Anthropologists also talk regularly of foundations and layers. It is not uncommon for those who support a combined biological/cultural approach, for example, to speak of culture as being built upon a biological foundation.

Perhaps most insightful and sophisticated are metaphors suggesting movement and transformation. Here there may be pathways, crossroads, and links. (In the next section I'll get to the bridges.) The image of a ship exploring an intellectual sea is also an interesting one. Discussing their work in a newly conceived "sociocultural psychology," Rosa and Valsiner (2007, 692) write, for example, that "A research field is indeed similar to a ship. It sails somewhere—sometimes only the direction may be known, but not the route, nor the harbor of arrival." Yet even with this you cannot avoid the geographical tropes. Even a sea of "open systems—biological, psychological, social, and epistemological—is always wrought with unexpected expansions into new areas of challenges" (ibid.).

Clearly, though, ship and sea metaphors need not always be so nice and positive. The weather and the waves are not always calm. In recent years, our anthropological ship has been facing some rough weather; we've been going through our own sea changes, although whether they represent tidal waves or dangers from oily seas depends on your perspective. For those who have feared the worst, talk has turned to breakages and threats to existence. Back in the mid-1990s, for example, noted British anthropologist Robin Fox argued that anthropology was becoming so fragmented that it was nearly in a "death grip" (Fox 1997, 196). Speaking more specifically about ethnography, the widely-cited ethnographer Bruce Kapferer argued more recently that "the postmodern movement in anthropology accentuated a rupture between the anthropology of the past and a reinvented anthropology more relevant to the times" such that there was the proverbial risk of "throwing the baby out with the bathwater" (Kapferer 2007, 189). At the extreme, critics from cultural anthropology have called four-field anthropology a "myth," "a noble lie," and have suggested it was just "sentimental." Most vociferous are the views of many of those who contributed to the volume by Daniel Segle and Sylvia Junko Yanagisako (2005). They find little value in biological perspectives and archaeology, seeing four-field unity not as a positive thing but as something that needs to be rejected. Indeed, such perspectives reflect literal divides, manifested publicly by the division of some prominent departments. Most notably, anthropology divided into cultural and biological wings at Duke (1988) and, a decade later, at Stanford. And there have been rumblings of a similar division at Harvard, with the actions for division this time apparently coming most from those with more biological interests (Shenk 2006). Still, this level of divisiveness may represent more of the statistical anomalies of the anthropological Rorschach than of the major trends. Stanford, for example, was reunited as a department in 2007. In addition to whatever epistemological reasons there may be for this, there are practical, generally budgetary, rationales for our continued unity as well. And, even division is not necessarily the "end of anthropology as we know it" as the split of a department does not necessarily mean a complete loss of four-field perspectives (Balée 2009). Nonetheless, the seriousness of the divide in anthropology should not be underestimated. More recently, for example, the executive board of the American Anthropological Association caused controversy by eliminating any reference to science from the association's mission statement (Berrett 2010).

As a matter of research, it has long been recognized that very few anthropologists are actually involved in study that combines the subfields (Balée 2009; Stocking 1988). Indeed, analysis by Rob Borofsky (2002) suggests that anthropologists rarely churn their research waters with material from other seas; his survey of 100 years of research published in the flagship journal *American Anthropologist* shows that fewer than 10 percent represented collaboration across the subfields. Apparently, even for those who maintain holism as an ideal, Boas and Kroeber have been rather more like mythic figures to be looked up to than model scholars to be emulated.

Still, I would argue that even if most of us do not have the time, the skills, or the inclination to work collaboratively across the fields, this does not invalidate the goal. Myth, in the sense of Malinowski, is an ideal and a charter for behavior. It does not have to be followed literally to be useful. And, as with ritual enactment, mythic enthusiasm may wax and wane. Indeed, things at the present historical moment do not look as divisive and lacking in unifying perspectives as they did in the 1990s. Perhaps we have weathered the most severe storms of our epistemological crisis and we are now facing calmer weather; and we are not just traveling to and from different ports. There are a number of trends in anthropological thought that are signs of this. In the next paragraph, I outline and reference at least eight types of studies that are being formulated by new understandings of nature-culture interactions.

First, the dichotomies between mind and brain, or mental and material, that have pervaded the discipline seem less certain in an era of functional MRIs and brain machine interfaces that allow thoughts to move robots (Blakeslee 2008). Second, the more wide-ranging but related contrasts formerly made between nature and nurture are less compelling when we take into consideration the potential impacts of nutrition, stress, and other environmental factors on gene expression and the possible long-term impacts of what is more broadly being termed *epigenetics* (Jablonka and Lamb 2006). Third, older notions of sociobiology that appeared to be over-reliant on reductionist representations of genes as selfish and models of all living things as individual maximizers have been modified by new empirical evidence demonstrating complexities such as epigenetic influences and evolution by symbiosis and modifications of the homeotic genes of embryological development. This rethinking extends also to the assumptions of neoclassical economics and the new field of behavioral economics, which itself has been demolishing the myth of the rationally calculating individual. Fourth, there are new developments in primatology, ranging from how chimpanzees and orangutans express significant cultural variability (Wrangham et al. 1996; van Schaik 2004; Langergraber et al. 2010) to how monkeys work more cooperatively and appear to be more content when receiving equitable rewards (Van Wolkenten 2007). Fifth, there are studies that indicate that evolved cognitive proclivities shape and limit forms of religious expression (Boyer 2002; Atran 2002; Barber, Wayland, and Barber 2004). Sixth, there is new emphasis on how we learn. For example, we seem to have evolved proclivities to imitate in terms of frequency and prestige that may create and foster apparent cultural maladaptations (Richerson and Boyd 2005). Also key here is the discovery of mirror neurons, specific neural networks first discovered in monkeys that unconsciously track the familiar behaviors of others. Seventh, instead of representing science as pure reductionism, there are more nuanced visions of nonlinear science and complexity (Deacon 2012; Delanda 2006; Mosko and Damon 2005; Kohring and Wynne-Jones 2007). Last, there is increasing study of how sociocultural and psychobiological processes interact to produce symbolic capacities and language. In one form, this concerns the perspective of embodied semantics, particularly, but not exclusively, about how language works by means of analogies that come from physical and bodily experience (Lakoff and Johnson 1999; Thibault 2006; Deacon 1998; Bickerton 2009). In another, archaeological, form it is about how a "symbolic mind" developed in prehistory from emergent processes of engagement with material artifacts (Renfrew 2008) and their metaphorical relations (Gamble 2007).

In a brief piece written for the *Bulletin of the General Anthropology Division of the American Anthropological Association*, Walter Goldschmidt suggests an image of anthropology that nicely captures a sense of the unity in complexity. This is the image of the bluebird and the nature of its coloration. Indeed, he suggests that anthropologists should adopt bluebirds as a kind of totem. He reasons as follows:

> There is no pigment in the bluebird's wing. Put a feather in a mortar and break it down and there is no blue stain but just a pile of grayish crumbs. The color, the very essence of what makes the bluebird so attractive, is made by the structure of the molecules on the feathers. The surface is made of crystals that reflect only blue light. It provides the perfect metaphor for what gives anthropology its brilliance. Our unique quality lies in the four-fold structure of our discipline; our brilliance is that when we speak, we reflect knowledge from the classic and troublesome four fields of our discipline. (2006, 1)

Here we have the description of a combination of factors that are similar to the ones that initially intrigued me about the inkblot image. There is a given structure, but it is seen differently from different perspectives. What is particularly intriguing about the bluebird image is the way it incorporates physical structure and a process of perception and interpretation. This gets us away from what Richardson and Hanebrink, in this volume, describe as the metaphors of geological layers and strata often used to represent the relationship between biology and culture. While culture must certainly depend on a biological foundation, in practice it is so intermeshed with this biological foundation that it appears more as the lustrous color of a feathered wing than as the sheen of a well-built house.

BUILDING BRIDGES: THE PAPERS

This volume consists of a set of 10 papers all but one of which was presented at the annual meeting of the Southern Anthropological Society (SAS) in Savannah, Georgia, in February of 2010. SAS was formed in the late 1960s primarily by cultural anthropologists based in the US South who wanted a regional organization that would be inclusive of the four-field approach, one that would be open to the participation of students and faculty alike. In 2010, the theme of the annual meeting was "Ports, Hubs and Bridges: Key Links in Anthropological Theory and Practice." The idea here was that in anthropology there are bridges and links worthy of discussion in a variety of ways. Important interconnections are to be found not only within the discipline, among the various types of anthropologies, but also between the anthropological professional and those others anthropologists teach, rely on for information, or otherwise focus on in their research.

It must be stated at the outset that the results of SAS's call to "talk bridge building" did not lead to a sudden change in the character of our meeting—as in the past, most of the papers were ethnographic or based on ethnographic accounts. Nonetheless, the theme did foster more across-the-subfields interaction than usual, and there were some interesting and unanticipated results of thinking of anthropology in terms of the metaphor of the bridge and the link. Following up on this, the papers in this volume elaborate upon bridges that can and have been built in theory, pedagogy, and practice, and in a variety of cultural contexts. They have been organized here into three groups. Part I consists of papers that emphasize theory and conceptual issues; part II is for papers about teaching and practice; and, part III is for papers with an ethnography focus.

Theory and Concepts

The three papers in this section represent quite different perspectives on the theme of anthropological interconnections, but they are also all about showing the interconnections between frameworks often divided. The first essay was solicited by the editor specifically for this volume because of the long commitment the first author, the late Miles Richardson, had to anthropological holism and because of his distinguished efforts to forge links between academics, students, and the general public. His death on November 14, 2011, was a great loss to the Southern Anthropological Society and to anthropology and humanism more generally. The paper "Traversing the Great Divide: The Embodiment of Discourse between You and Me," which Richardson developed with his former student Julia Hanebrink, is characteristic of Richardson's style in that it combines logical insight and zest for all things anthropological and philosophical with poetic flair and good humor. Its key point is that we are simultaneously biological and cultural beings and that the divides we may feel as individuals mask a deeper interconnection between the psychological and the social. There is much food for thought here even in this brief essay; the interested reader may delve more deeply into these issues by perusing Richardson's (2006) *Being-in-Christ and Putting Death in Its Place: An Anthropologist's Account of Christian Performance in Spanish America and the American South*, which, despite its title, contains much about biological anthropology and an evolutionary perspective.

In "Culture as Information: Not a Shaky Link but a Stable Connection," I briefly discuss what I believe to be a neglected conceptualization of culture, that of culture-as-information. This perspective has an advantage in that links and flows across borders are as anticipated as boundary-making barriers. In particular, I stress several bridge-building features of this view of culture. These include that information processes pervade life, and perhaps even physical processes, and that an information perspective can foster a less anthropocentric and more naturalistic approach to the discipline without being essentialist. Provided that one sees these processes as emergent and synergistic rather than reductionist, one need not rely on the static geological metaphors that Richardson and Hanebrink critique.

In his article "Human Scales," Thomas Brasdefer considers another major issue, that of the role of scale in the social sciences, and takes up venerable questions about the relationship between maps and territories and how to link or network the scales of small, medium, and large, and all in between. Quite rightly, he argues that a proper understanding of how scaling works is necessary if we want to retain the possibility of valid generalization without ignoring the investigation of the details of the unique. Brasdefer provides a history of debates about scale in human geography, ethnography, and sociolinguistics and concludes with a brief case study relating these issues to policies concerning Native American languages. While his interests are primarily historical and ethnographic, a sense of scale that takes into consideration the local while still taking into account the global is clearly a concern for many other types of analysis.

Teaching and Practice

Teaching and engaging the broader community in anthropological perspectives have probably never been more important than they are today. Taking this into account, in this volume there are four papers that concern teaching and practice. The first is an in-depth assessment of college student interpretations of religion and evolution. The next two concern particular methods for teaching and practice, with the second being primarily archaeological but also highly interdisciplinary and the third being focused on teaching students about the contemporary situation of a particular place in Africa. The fourth paper concerns the production and dissemination of ethnographically informed film geared toward fostering positive social change.

In "I Didn't Evolve From No Monkey: Religious Narratives About Human Evolution in the US Southeast," H. Lyn White Miles and Christopher Marinello describe some of their findings from a 12-year-long investigation into student attitudes about evolution and religious cosmology at the University of Tennessee. They report here analysis of the responses to one particular survey item made by a subsample of 846 students, with 759 narrative explanations (from a total sample of 4,662 students). In this item, students chose among statements that gave them five perspectives about evolution and religion on a "creationism-naturalistic evolution" continuum and then were asked to provide a written justification of their response. In line with other studies, Miles and Marinello find substantial resistance to change of deeply held, historically ingrained, worldviews; and, indeed, fewer incoming students now accept the scientific facts of evolution than did a mere decade or two ago. Newer to this study is the focus on how attitudes toward evolution reflect students' intellectual development and senses of certainty. Among the findings are that "nearly two thirds of students gave flat one-sided statements or

acknowledged the other side of the issue but made no attempt to relate their choices to their identity, major, or understanding of science
or religion." While a majority accepted the facts of evolution, many
were comfortable rejecting prehistory and other ancient history with
the justification that scientific evidence could be a complete fabrica-
tion. We may also note here that such a disconnect between evidence
and belief is probably not unrelated to the large gap found between
scientific knowledge in other areas and what is generally believed in
popular culture, such as beliefs about the realities of the global environment and climate (Elrich 2002, 5-6; Elrich 2010). More recently,
a "back fire effect" has also been reported whereby exposure to facts
that contradict one's worldview may have the ironic effect of actually
strengthening that worldview (Nyhan and Reifler 2010). In discussing this research, Miles and Marinello also provide details on how
they use their results to more effectively teach about evolution in the
classroom.

Because of its complex nature, the next paper, "Enculturating
Student Anthropologists Through Fieldwork in Fiji," is given more
space than others in the volume. Written by a team that includes
professors and students, this paper is really a set of papers within a
paper. The first section describes the nature of a rather extraordinary
model of interdisciplinary collaboration in pedagogy and research.
Based in part on the project called MATRIX, "Making Archaeology
Teaching Relevant in the XXI Century," the project involved University of Alabama at Birmingham students and professors working
together to develop a field school to investigate the prehistory and
ethnoarchaeology of marine resource use on four islands of the Lau
group in Fiji. In the first year of the project, both undergraduates and
graduates did research in archaeology, ethnoarchaeology, ethnography, and history relating to garbology, toponomy, foodways, traditional knowledge systems, and environmental/ecological change;

and their initial findings are given in separate sections here. All this demonstrates that the project is not only a great model for interdisciplinary teaching and research but for the practical application of that knowledge as well.

In the next paper, "Making Africa Accessible: Bringing Guinea-Bissau into the University Classroom," Brandon D. Lundy focuses attention on how he works in the classroom to overcome misperceptions about Africa and on the techniques he employs to engage students in the kind of understanding that comes from rich ethnographic experience. The paper thereby represents a good example of how anthropological reflexivity—learning about yourself in the process of learning about another—can be put to use in motivating students to feel a sense of connection to others, particularly others who are too often ignored in the popular media or portrayed in terms of negative or distancing stereotypes.

With the paper "Causes Mini-Film Festival: Anthropology for Public Consumption" by Matthew Richard and Andrea Zvikas, the focus of the papers shifts to public education and issue advocacy. It describes the development of a mini-film festival that had been created in recent years by Matthew Richard and his students at Valdosta State University. In this paper, the authors show how the festival brings together the skills of fine-grained ethnographic observation with fine-grained filmmaking. The films screened are self-written and produced and no more than 90 seconds in length, and they have the goal of focusing on a particular social problem or issue of concern to a local community. On the one hand, as Richard puts it, making such films gives students the "opportunity to apply their developing understanding of social forces in order to bring about transformation in our society." On the other hand, the very success of the Causes festival indicates that others outside the student base are also getting involved in the use of film to stimulate awareness of issues and thereby to foster positive change.

Ethnographic Emphasis

Part III has papers that are location-specific ethnographies. They reflect some of the diversity of ethnographic approaches that one can find today in anthropology but also show linkages between different research areas, worldviews, and particular theoretical concerns. The first paper is set among Pentecostals in Guatemala, the second among the human visitors to a Florida zoo, and the third among students in Japan. In terms of topics, one is about understanding the meaning and form of Christian religious practice today, one is about adult and children's perceptions of apes, and one is about the nuances of a linguistic concept in Japan.

C. Mathews Samson's paper, "Searching for the Spirit: Researching Spirit-Filled Religion in Guatemala," is the work of a seasoned ethnographer who has devoted years of his life to the study of a sociocultural phenomenon that is both local and transnational. As in other parts of Latin America and the world, Guatemala has seen a rapid growth in Protestant denominations that are often known under such labels as Pentecostal, Charismatic, or Renewal in the Holy Spirit. Taking his cue from the work of Bruce Lincoln, who sees religion and religious institutions as more nuanced and flexible than they are often given credit for, Samson finds that members of the "Full Gospel Church of God," among whom he has worked in Guatemala, cannot be characterized simply as inward-looking and otherworldly. Rather, they are involved in particular forms of networking and bridge building in their own way. And here "the ethnographic stance is one in which the ethnographic lens becomes a bridge between one culture and another, sometimes serving as a bridge for cross-cultural, and even intercultural understanding."

In the paper with the most peculiar title here, "Ooo Ooo, Aah Aah," I offer a brief analysis of the types of things children and adults say while watching bonobos and other primates at the zoo. I suggest that the conversations people have with each other about the apes and the observational statements people make about ape behavior and appearance reflect both unconscious, mostly accurate, identifications with the animals and projections onto them of commonly understood human behaviors and attributes. In this, there are two major patterns, which I label "Mirrored Behavioral Analogies" and "Misconceived Interpretive Schemas." The paper also hypothesizes a biological basis for a projection (or, more precisely, mapping) of human body and behavioral schemas to bonobo body and behavioral schemas.

Undergraduate students often have opportunities to do locally based fieldwork only, with their ethnographic observations taking place near their homes or schools. But students come from diverse backgrounds and have differing travel opportunities. Lauren Levine's paper here is based on her experiences as an exchange student during a nine-month period in Nagoya, Japan. It focuses on trying to understand what linguistic anthropologist Michael Agar has termed a "rich point," a cross-cultural difference that is not easy to frame in the familiar terms of one's native tongue. Given the bridge-building theme, "The Kegare Concept" is a particularly rich concept to attempt to link or translate. Do the Japanese understandings of *kegare* equate to Western senses of "pollution," "cleanliness," and "propriety"? Is the concept employed in same way among students today as it was in traditional Japan? Or, is it better to understand kegare in terms of the meta-analysis of human concepts of pollution put forth by Mary Douglas and others? As is typical with other conceptually rich points, the answer given here is not "Yes or No" but "yes and no." To begin to unravel what kegare is all about one needs to think in terms of various domains. Kegare is peculiarly Japanese, but it is also linked to universal ways of thinking. It is reflective of tradition, but it is also reflective of our changing times. Interestingly enough for a volume about links, study of kegare (and thinking back to the findings of Douglas) reminds us that combing categories previously kept distinct often makes many people feel uncomfortable.

REFERENCES

Atran, Scott. 2002. *In Gods We Trust: The Evolutionary Landscape of Religion*. New York: Oxford University Press.

Balée, William. 2009. "The Four-Field Model of Anthropology in the United States." *Amazônica–Revista de Antropologia* 1(1). http://www.periodicos.ufpa.br/index.php/amazonica/article/view/136/207.

Barber, Elizabeth Wayland and Paul T. Barber. 2004. *When They Severed Earth from Sky: How the Human Mind Shapes Myth*. Princeton: Princeton University Press.

Berrett, Dan. 2010. "Anthropology without Science." *Inside Higher Education*, November. http://www.insidehighered.com/news/2010/11/30/anthroscience.

Bickerton, Derek. 2009. *Adam's Tongue: How Humans Made Language, How Language Made Humans*. New York: Hill and Wang.

Blakeslee, Sandra. 2008. "Monkey's Thoughts Propel Robot, A Step that May Help Humans." *New York Times*, January 15. http://www.nytimes.com/2008/01/15/science/15robo.html.

Borofsky, Rob. 2002. "The Four Subfields: Anthropologists as Mythmakers." *American Anthropologist* 104(2):463-480.

Boyer, Pascal. 2002. *Religion Explained: The Evolutionary Origins of Religious Thought*. New York: Basic Books.

Deacon, Terrance. 1998. *The Symbolic Species: The Co-Evolution of Language and the Brain*. New York: Norton.

———. 2012. *Incomplete Nature: How Mind Emerged from Matter*. New York: Norton.

Delanda, Manuel. 2006. *A New Philosophy of Society: Assemblage Theory and Social Complexity*. New York: Continuum.

Elrich, Paul R. 2002. *Human Natures: Genes, Cultures, and the Human Project*. New York: Penguin.

———. 2010. "The MAHB, the Culture Gap, and Some Really Inconvenient Truths." *PLoS Biology* 8(4)1-3.

Fox, Robin. 1997. *Conjectures and Confrontation: Science, Evolution, Social Concern*. New Brunswick, NJ: Transaction Books.

Gamble, Clive. 2007. *Origins and Revolutions: Human Identity in Earliest Prehistory*. Cambridge: Cambridge University Press.

Goldschmidt, Walter. 2006. "Anthropology: The Bluebird People." *Bulletin of the General Anthropology Division* 13(2):1, 9-11.

Iacoboni, Marco. 2008. *Mirroring People: The New Science of How We Connect with Others*. New York: Farrar, Straus and Giroux.

Jablonka, Eva and Marion J. Lamb. 2006. *Evolution in Four Dimensions: Genetic, Epigenetic, Behavioral, and Symbolic Variation in the History of Life*. Cambridge, MA: MIT Press.

Kapferer, Bruce. 2007. "Afterword." In *Holding Worlds Together: Ethnographies of Knowing and Belonging*, edited by Mariann Elisabeth Lien and Marit Melhuus, 185-198. New York: Berghahn Books.

Kohring, Sheila, and Stephanie Wynne-Jones, eds. 2007. *Socializing Complexity: Approaches to Power and Interaction in the Archaeological Record*. London: Oxbow Books.

Lakoff, George and Mark Johnson. 1999. *Philosophy in the Flesh: The Embodied Mind and Its Challenge to Western Thought.* New York: Basic Books.

Langergraber, Kevin E., Christophe Boesch, Eiji Inoue, et al. 2010. "Genetic and 'Cultural' Similarity in Wild Chimpanzees." *Proceedings of Royal Society B.* http://rspb.royalsociety publishing.org/content/early/2010/08/10/rspb.2010.1112.

Mosko, Mark S., and Frederick H. Damon, eds. 2005. *On the Order of Chaos: Social Anthropology and the Science of Chaos.* New York: Berghahn.

Nyhan, Brendan and Jason Reifler. 2010. "When Corrections Fail: The Persistence of Political Misperceptions." *Political Behavior* 32(2):303-330.

Renfrew, Colin. 2008. "Neuroscience, Evolution and the Sapient Paradox: The Factuality of Value and of the Sacred." *Philosophical Transactions of the Royal Society of London B* 363: 2041-2047.

Richardson, Miles. 2006. *Being-in-Christ and Putting Death in Its Place: An Anthropologist's Account of Christian Performance in Spanish America and the American South.* Baton Rouge: Louisiana State University Press.

Richerson, Peter J., and Robert Boyd. 2005. *Not by Genes Alone: How Culture Transformed Human Evolution.* Chicago: University of Chicago Press.

Rosa, Alberto, and Jaan Valsiner. 2007. "Socio-cultural Psychology on the Move: Semiotic Methodology in the Making." In *The Cambridge Handbook of Sociocultural Psychology,* edited by Jaan Valsiner and Alberto Rosa, 692-707. Cambridge: Cambridge University Press.

Segal, Daniel, and Sylvia Junko Yanagisako, eds. 2005. *Unwrapping the Sacred Bundle: Reflections on the Disciplining of Anthropology*. Durham: Duke University Press.

Shenk, Mary K. 2006. "Models for the Future of Anthropology." *Anthropology News*. January 6-7.

Stocking, George. 1988. "Guardians of the Sacred Bundle: The American Anthropological Association and the Representation of Holistic Anthropology." In *Learned Societies and the Evolution of the Disciplines*, edited by S.B. Cohen, D. Bromwich, and G.W. Stocking, Jr. ACLS *Occasional Paper* 5, 17-25. New York: American Council of Learned Societies.

Thibault, Paul. 2006. *Brain, Mind and the Signifying Body: An Ecosocial Semiotic Theory*. London: Continuum.

Van Shaik, Carel, and Perry van Duijnhoven. 2004. *Among Orangutans: Red Apes and the Rise of Human Culture*. Harvard: Harvard University Press.

Van Wolkenten, M., S. Brosnan, and F. de Waal. 2007. "Inequity Responses of Monkeys Modified by Effort." *Proceedings of the National Academy of Sciences* 104(47):18854-18859.

Wrangham, Richard W., W.C. McGrew, Frans B. M. de Waal, and Paul Heltne, eds. 1996. *Chimpanzee Cultures*. Harvard: Harvard University Press.

PART I
Theory and Concepts

Traversing the Great Divide: The Embodiment of Discourse Between You and Me

Miles Richardson and Julia Hanebrink

In considering how we, you and I, are, we must abandon the ancient dichotomy that would divide us separately into two geology layers, the bottom one labeled *biology* and the top one called culture. Instead, we must recognize that we need each other to be, and we must recognize also that we are what we are, creatures of flesh and blood who speak to one another and to others. Viewed thusly we, you and I, are never out of "culture" nor out of "biology." We are whole, though unfinished, beings. With all due respect to Descartes, we are not I's who think our separate selves into existence, but in order to be we must be you and I, with you primary. You are, consequently I am. The others outside of the we world are the mysterious they. The they are also evil. We ask at the end, what is the source of the they's evil?

TRAVERSING THE GREAT DIVIDE

The following text comes largely from a manuscript, "Hominid Evolution: The Trajectory of You and Me." We, Miles and Julia, intend that the larger manuscript will be a six-chapter attempt to lodge humans in the life process, destination Mars!

Thomas Huxley, known as "Darwin's Bulldog" for his tenacious defense of Charles Darwin and a widely recognized comparative anatomist in his own right, published in 1902 *Man's Place in Nature.*

On the very first page he posed "the question of questions" (1902, 77): What is our place in nature? Today at the beginning of the twenty-first century, the question of questions still haunts us. Despite insightful responses (Tomasello 1999; Shennan 2002; Janson and Smith 2003; Richerson and Boyd 2006; and especially Odling-Smee et al. 2003), the haunting continues, and, despite years of personal struggle, this effort here will surely *not* lay the ghost (the demon!) to rest.

In addressing such a question, we must *transcend* that hoary dichotomy that persists in speaking of us as a geological formation, with the culture stratum lying noncomfortably atop and, consequently, independent of the underlying biological stratum. Addressed in the honesty of now, are we not two flesh and blood creatures speaking this text into being? I by writing and you by reading? If so, then we are *not* basically *god* (symbol) with a daub of embarrassing ape, nor essentially *ape* (DNA) dressed in an ephemeral gown of culture. We are whole (though unfinished!) creatures, engaged in the open struggle to be whatever and whoever we are.

A view of the evolutionary process from the origin of life on this planet until the now of you and me brings into view the intricate linkage through which we come about and by which we make our way. We, you and I, are emergent. We depend upon each other to be. True of us; true of life. Since its beginnings on this planet, some 3.5 billion years ago, life has implicated itself in its own development. True of life; true of us. Narrating the evolutionary process is the closest we anthropologists may ever come to a reckoning of what humans are about. This is especially the case as we now realize we are not the triumphal, final link in the "Great Chain of Being," but instead, "a minor twig on a ragged old eucalyptus" (Graves 2003, 1621).

"Closest," however, is nowhere near near. Yet "the evolutionary epic is … the best myth we will ever have," [one that meets the] "mythopoetic requirements of the mind" (Wilson 1978, 109); that is, one that grabs us. (See Figure 1.1.)

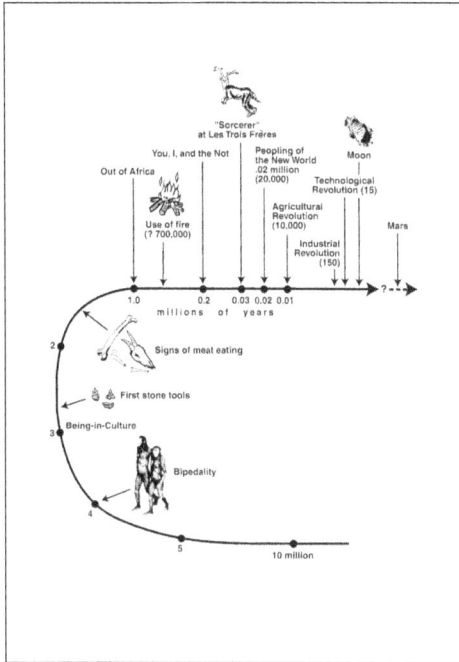

Figure 1.1. The hominid-human mythopoetic trajectory of us

In his masterful *The Symbolic Species*, Terrence Deacon culminates his 452-page analysis with, "It is simply not possible to understand human anatomy, human neurobiology, or human psychology without recognizing they have been shaped by ... symbolic reference" (1997, 410). Consequently, symbol-communication stands not apart from nature and life processes but is intertwined within it.

To depict the intertwining challenges our metaphoric skills. The geological metaphor that anthropologists have developed has a cultural stratum sitting in geological language incongruously atop a biological stratum, as in Figure 1.2.

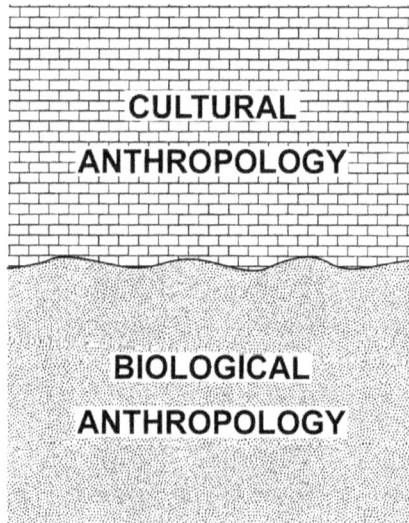

Figure 1.2. Culture sitting on top of nature

Figure 1.3 abandons the geological, horizontal metaphor for a more social, vertical aesthetic. It declares we are never all "Nature;" neither are we ever independent of "Culture." The darker the black, the greater the intertwining between biology and culture. As we move toward the edges of the drawing, vertically or horizontally, the black lightens; *however*, nowhere are we out of the black. As Jacques Derrida would say, "There is nothing outside the text." Similarly, Theodosius Dobzhansky might add, "There is nothing outside of evolution." Nowhere in the figure are we less human or more human. We are equally human, top-to-bottom and side-to-side. Similarly, we are never frozen monads. Male and female, You–I, together, constitute *us*, basic humanity. Being bound to each, how is it that we figure what each is up to? Tricky business this bounding. In the sensory, mammalian sense, we are bound as penis is to vagina, as embryo to uterus, and as lip to nipple, but the symbol, semiotic sense, we are bound as You to Me, as one arbitrary, deictic sign to another. Thus, a distance separates the two figures in figure 1.3, an arbitrary distance of impossible loneliness.

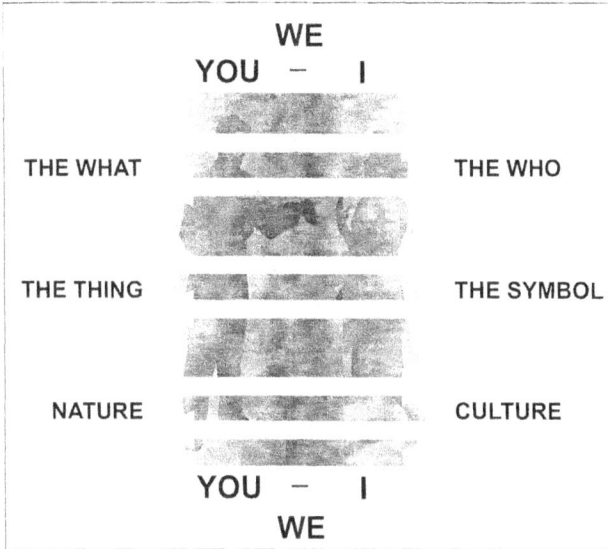

Figure 1.3. Culture-nature, you-I

Phenomenologically, we cross, or pretend to do so, the two figures through understanding. (For elegant interpretations, see Csordas 1993, Kerdeman 1998, and Macquarrie 1994.)

We must see understanding as action. As human action, understanding is "*socioculturally mediated*" (Ahearn 2001, 112; our emphasis). By understanding each other, we bring about a co-presence that transcends the dichotomy of raw experience and pure sign. In our everyday mode of being, understanding and sense perception go hand in hand. It is available to us through its materiality, in the materiality of intersubjective exchanges, out there, *not* in here.

To summarize: Culture is symbol-communication. It is not a thing located in our individual heads, but discourse in the widest sense, including body movements and material objects crafted by the hand. These objects range from pebble tools to the space station; they are a part of the world we create, and whatever their function, they define our presence, our be-ing.

This brings us to you and me.

In considering the world that we construct with symbol-communication we must recall what we often even *want* to forget: that we, you and I, are *embedded* in that world. That world cannot exist apart from us, nor we apart from the world. As Tulane professor Arden King insisted years ago, "Miles, you must keep phenomena whole." Now, finally, I understand what he meant. I suggest that the concept that best achieves the tie between our world and us is "being-in-the-world." The concept comes from Martin Heidegger's *Being and Time* (1996). The hyphens indicate that being-in-the-world is unitary. For us, for you and me, to exist, we must have a world to be in. The world that we are in is the world of symbol-communication. Nowhere today, and not since the emergence of the australopithecine grade, more than 2.5 million years ago, can you find a bipedal primate who does not communicate in symbols. The important "kicker" is that the world we must have in order to be, *we create*. The "being" in "being-in-the-world" is not a noun but a gerund, a verbal, a "be-ing"

As implied in the "we," being-in-the-world is social. If I may be so bold to say, Descartes had it wrong when he famously said, "I think, therefore I am." Correctly put, "You are, therefore so am I." Thus we, you and I, are not only dialogically paired, but you are primary. Just as this text awaits your reading, without you I cannot be.

Guided by Heidegger and propelled by the desire to "keep phenomena whole," this venture of replacing the individual organism with you and me also draws strong support from two major phenomenologists, Stephan Strasser and Alfred Schutz. Strasser wrote in *The Idea of Dialogal* (sic) *Phenomenology*. "The 'you' does not come into my world; it is *already* there, for the 'you' is <u>older</u> than I. More precisely speaking, we should say that the "you" is *already* a "you" with respect to me *before* I am an Ego" (1969, 52 [emphasis added]). Schutz likewise argues that not only in our everyday world, the pared bond, you-I, is primary, but you-I, the we, precedes both the lonely I and the objective, mysterious they (Schutz 1966).

Mentioning the "lonely I and the objective, mysterious they" requires further elaboration. The lonely I is indeed a tragic figure. Despite his or her searches, neither can find a you that will bring them about. I need you to come about, to be. But what if I cannot find you? I cannot be myself without you, but you are nowhere around. I have searched without success. The world is full of yous: pretty ones, ugly ones, rich ones, poor ones, smart ones, dumb ones, refined ones, redneck ones. But you I cannot find. I'm lonely; "I'm so lonesome I could cry." But what the hell? It's not the first time you have disappeared on me. So here are two poems just for you.

Ain't It The Truth!

You say that love multiplies,
   that it doubles itself
   every twenty years.

You say that love conquers,
   that it triumphs in face
   of overwhelming odds.

You say that love endures,
   that it lasts forever,
   and is, in fact, eternal.

You say ... well, you say
   a lot of things.

How Is It Where You Live?

I reach for you.
You reach for me.
We touch…
when it doesn't rain,
and it's not too hot.

Here, in Louisiana,
that ain't often.

What about the "objective, mysterious they"? They are always over there, never here. They, like you and I, are devoid of gender. They, you, and I could be feminine or masculine. Nothing in their pronoun-hood gives you a hint. They, however, pack in the shes and hes. The partner to they, them, fills up with hers and hises. So they, the both of them, contain their gender within. Perhaps that explains the mystery of the mysterious they. You don't know until it is too late, but whamo! a change in a verb and a she pops up, or a he un-furls. Much to the they's disgust. He or she opens the possibility that one or the other is responsible to what transpires, as in "He hit the ball." "She hit him." The they can never be responsible, even if "They slaughter hundreds," as in the holocaust. You never find a he who says, "I killed them all." The they forever remain they. The real mystery of they is in "they say." You don't know who is saying. It could be anyone, but likely it is nobody. Heidegger calls that they the they-self, a self everyone recognizes but no one knows. In any discussion of death, a favorite expression is "They say we all have to go sometime." How many times have I heard that? How many times have you said it?

The they remains anonymous, and perhaps that is the source of they's power.

Have you ever thought that the they resembles Christ?

No I have not, but I'm sure you have got to tell us.

In the common expression "Christ saves," doesn't that sound a lot like the they, an all encompassing endeavor?

Stop taking pot shots at Christians.

Let us continue our discussion of I, you, we, and they. Used as a throwaway word, "we" can assume some of the all encompassing features of they, as in "We Americans believe in liberty." In that common statement, I and you can safely hide in the we's anonymity. That is the reason I constantly insist that we are you and I. Since we always means you and I, we, you and I, assume responsibility for our actions.

We always stand in opposition to they. In that opposition, frequently they comes off worse. True we say they are a friendly group, but how much more common is it that we don't like them? The reasons for our dislike run almost without end: They smell bad, they can't be trusted, they steal anything that is not nailed down, they threaten our women, they scrimp on whatever job you give them, and in brief they are trifling and no good. If any one is foolish enough to defend them, we can always point to specific traits or even cases to support our argument. We become righteous in our condemnation, and so they take on evil into their makeup, in their character. We feel more and more the obligation to destroy them, so as to make the world safe and secure for all peace-loving people.

And then someone, you, asks us to examine our conscience. I may challenge your motives. But bless you, you are strong and persist.

Your courage will take us to the unbelievable question: Are we the source of the they's evil?

And with that question ringing in our ears, yours and mine, I can do no more than stop. Thank you for your careful reading.

EDITOR'S NOTE

Miles Richardson (1932-2011) was one of the founding members of
the Southern Anthropological Society (SAS). In developing this paper at the editor's request, Miles wanted to note for the record that
SAS was founded in a two-step process. First, in the spring of 1966,
a group of anthropologists at the meeting of the Southern Sociological Society in New Orleans voted unanimously to form a separate
society of anthropologists. Second, the first meeting of the society
was held in Atlanta the following spring, 1967. The name Southern
Anthropological Society was chosen to distinguish the group from
the existing Southeast Archaeological Conference, but also with the
intention that it would be inclusive of the traditional four-fields. As
Miles put it, there was uniform consent that the acronym SAS "expressed well the feeling of this upstart society."

REFERENCES

Ahearn, Laura M. 2001. "Language and Agency." *Annual Review of
     Anthropology* 30:109-137.

Buber, Martin. 1958. *The I and Thou*. New York: Scribner.

Csordas, Thomas J. 1993. "Somatic Modes of Attention." *Cultural
     Anthropology* 8:135-156.

Deacon, Terrance. 1997. *The Symbolic Species: The Co-evolution of
     Language and the Brain*. New York: W. W. Norton.

Graves, Jennifer A. Marshal. 2003. "The Tree of Life: View from a
     Twig." *Science* 300:1621.

Heidegger, Martin. 1996. *Being and Time: A Translation of Sein und
     Zeit*. Translated by Joan Stambaugh. Albany, New York:
     State University of New York Press.

Huxley, Thomas H. 1902. *Man's Place in Nature*. New York: H. L. Fowle.

Janson, Charles and Eric A. Smith, eds. 2003. "The Evolution of Culture: New Perspectives and Evidence." *Evolutionary Anthropology* 12:57-105.

Kerdeman, Deborah. 1998. "Hermeneutics and Education: Understanding, Control, and Agency." *Educational Theory* 48:241-266.

Macquarrie, John. 1994. *Heidegger and Christianity*. New York: Contiuum.

Odling-Smee, F. John, et al. 2003. *Niche Construction: The Neglected Process in Evolution*. Princeton: Princeton University Press.

Richerson, Peter J., and Robert Boyd. 2006. *Not by Genes Alone: How Culture Transformed Human Evolution*. Chicago: University of Chicago.

Schutz, Alfred. 1966. *Collected Papers III*. The Hague: Martinus Nijhoff.

Shennan, Stephen J. 2002. *Genes, Memes and Human History: Darwinian Archaeology and Cultural Evolution*. London: Thames and Hudson.

Strasser. Stephan. 1969. *The Idea of Dialogal* (sic) *Phenomenology*. Pittsburgh: Duquesne University Press.

Strauss, Anselm, ed. 1964. *George Herbert Mead on Social Psychology*. Chicago: University of Chicago Press.

Tomasello, Michael. 1999. "The human adaptation for culture." *Annual Review of Anthropology* 28:509-552.

Wilson, Edward O. 1978. *On Human Nature*. Cambridge: Harvard University Press.

Culture as Information: Not a Shaky Link but a Stable Connection

Robert Shanafelt

Who has not heard debates in which esteemed scholars fight over whether we should modify the culture concept, reclaim it, or just throw it out? I suggest that a major sector in a bridge between fields of anthropology has already been partially constructed, but what has been built has been too much under the radar. This construction links a conception of culture with that of information.

It seems that a definition of culture in terms of information has not received the benefit of much historical and critical analysis. Here I will provide a little history as well as advocate for a particular perspective that I see as most fruitful for a synthesizing anthropology. I will also outline some key work from this perspective and discuss some of its strengths and weaknesses. My argument is that the pitfalls of the other conceptualizations of culture involving reductionism and dualism can be sidestepped by a better understanding of information and its forms and processes.[1]

Although some have suggested that we should leave all our worry about culture behind (Fox and King 2002), I think the concept of culture is still worth talking about because definitions have consequences and the modifications we make to them reflect our changing interests and concerns. Of course, with so many variations on the theme of culture, oftentimes changes may be minor and go unnoticed. Sometimes, however, they do reflect major shifts in perspective. In the 1990s, for example, Susan Wright (1998) argued that one could divide the culture concept into "old" and "new" versions. The old version, she thought, "equates 'a culture' with 'a people' who could be delineated with a boundary and a checklist of characteristics" (14); the newer version saw culture as a "contested process of meaning-making" (9).

Undoubtedly the more recent trends reflect the influence and prestige of prominent exemplars such as Clifford Geertz and Michael Foucault, although, of course, emphasis on meaning and the relativism of perspectives did not originate with them. Most probably, the recent attentions to issues of power and its contestation owe more to Foucault than Geertz, and certainly some is due to Eric Wolf and the "old" Neo-Marxians as well. In this paper, however, I am not inclined to critique these trends. Here I have the more modest goal of following a relatively unexamined definition to see where it has led and to make a few comments about where it might lead. While culture-as-information has been quietly advocated for some time now by a few scholars, it is not remarked upon as often as are others. It is not mentioned in Kroeber and Kluckhohn's (1952) classic overview or in Keesing's (1974) review, for example; nor is it delineated in a more recent comprehensive, interdisciplinary, survey of the term's use (Baldwin et al. 2006). In the early 1970s, Bohannan (1973) did suggest that culture be seen as "a mode of encoding information," but he provided very little historical background or epistemological foundation for his argument.

There are three things that strike me most about the potentials of a view of culture as information that are immediately worth noting. First, such a view can help foster a less anthropocentric approach to the discipline. This is true in that information and information processes pervade life. Second, for the same reason—the pervasiveness of information—this perspective can help foster a link between

anthropology and natural sciences. Third, a view of culture as information can help mitigate concerns about reification and boundaries.
This is the case because information moves between boundaries, and
attempts to contain it require expressions of power that are often difficult to hide. Clearly, although information perspectives on culture
are not new, in Wright's sense, they also do not necessarily have the
negative characteristics of the old ones she describes. And they are
in keeping with newer models that see social institutions as "assemblages" constituted by relations between interior and exterior conditions and entropic and tropic forces (Delanda 2006).

With respect to boundaries, it may be of interest to note that I
first became aware of information perspectives while studying the
anthropology of South Africa. I learned from this that other more
standard anthropological definitions of culture did not seem contrary to apartheid notions of group boundedness and that they even
helped obscure the interconnections that existed between all of the
racial and ethnic groups living together in the country. The information perspective described by Robert Thornton (1988) did not seem
to have these problems.

I do not mean to imply that an information perspective on culture is without problems. Three commonly suggested complaints
with informational views immediately come to mind. First is that
the information models derived from computers and telecommu-
nications have tended toward a philosophical dualism, implying a
stark contrast between information stored in the head and information sent or received from exterior sources. Another problem is that
this perspective of information as coded transmission does not get
at the problem of meaning. This is particularly evident in the mathematical perspective of Shannon and Weaver (1949), wherein one
sees information only as signals or average options among all possibilities, irrespective of what specific message they convey. While the

mathematical theory of information has been extremely fruitful in a developing technology, such a perspective is contrary to our ordinary sense of information as "about being informed." A third and related problem is that informational views can be mechanistic and may therefore neglect the creative and synergistic features of shared communications. Cultural communications are not simply downloaded from society to the individual or uploaded from the individual to the society. As Durkheim realized long ago, there is a "public temper" to social communication that involves the creation of new meaning in the process of interaction (Durkheim 1933, 102).

With respect to scholarly exemplars, Gregory Bateson and Claude Lèvi-Strauss should be included in any history of information-as-culture in that they wrote in terms of cybernetics, communication theory, messages, and codes. Of course, Bateson developed his concept of information as "any difference that makes a difference" in the context of a broad interdisciplinary perspective while Lèvi-Strauss was interested in decoding hidden cultural structures. Less influential has been the research agenda developed by ethnographer John M. Roberts, starting in the 1940s, that focused on the description of culture as an information resource (Roberts 1964; Roberts 1987). Roberts concentrated his efforts on analysis of the relationship between the cultural knowledge of individuals and small groups and the combined pool of information available to all members of a society. Another prominent anthropologist, Ward Goodenough, wrote in a similar vein about culture and individuals accessing the "information pool" of a society (Goodenough 1954). Although both Goodenough and Roberts were students of George Peter Murdock at Yale, according to Goodenough's (2003) recollection, their focus on information pools does not seem to be due to Murdock's influence.

The 1940s saw a surge of interdisciplinary interest in cybernetics and Shannon and Weavers' probabilistic perspective that also influenced many anthropologists. In archaeology, an explicit link was made to this by David Clarke (1978) when he developed a cybernetic approach to archaeological theory. According to Clive Gamble (1986, 56), by the mid-1980s the idea of culture as an information system was already considered a commonplace archaeological view. However, more recently this seems to have gone out of fashion. Gamble (2007) himself, for example, has moved on to an emphasis on a kind of "embodied semantics of the artifact" that reflects the influence of linguist George Lakoff and his colleagues (although in this a relational view of information processes remains implicit).

In zoology and biological anthropology, an informational definition was given a prominent place by John Bonner (1980, 9) who wrote in *The Evolution of Culture in Animals* that culture is "the transfer of information by behavioral means, most particularly by the process of teaching and learning." Bonner's influence continues in anthropology and other areas that highlight evolutionary perspectives. For example, primatologists Duane Quiatt and Vernon Reynolds (1993, 46) define culture in a way similar to that of Bonner, describing it as "socially processed information, a definable subset of the environment (as opposed to genetically encoded) information which is accessible to a given species." A related definition has been employed for some decades now by the theorists of cultural evolution, Robert Boyd and Peter J. Richerson (1985; see also Richerson and Boyd 2006) as well as by William Durham (2002, 194). Charles D. Laughlin, an anthropologist who had proclaimed the culture concept dead in 1972 (Freilich 1989, 1), has more recently worked to bring it back to life by placing emphasis on information in the context of research into what he calls "cultural neurophenomenology" (Laughlin and Throop 2006).[2] In an edited volume featuring both the works of Goodenough and of Boyd and Richerson, Morris Freilich (1989) gives the most prominent emphasis to informational definitions of culture (one third of the book) that I am aware of in any anthropological study on the subject.

Looking at culture in terms of information, of course, begs the question as to what information is. Since in this volume we are interested in implications for anthropological synthesis, what is most germane are the most discipline-bending notions of information. These are not difficult to find. Indeed, since Leo Szilard's (1929) solution to the problem of Maxwell's demon in thermodynamics, the processing of information has been known to have an energetic cost. Some natural scientists have even gone so far as to argue that information is a "fundamental universal phenomena alongside and related to matter and energy" (Young 1987, 2; see also Weiner 1948). Along the same lines, ecologist Ramon Margalef has argued that information is a property of "everything that is formed of distinct parts" (Adams 1988, 41, quoting and translating a line from Margalef's 1980 work in Spanish, *La biosfera*). Obviously, if this is true, then information is not something ethereal. Put in the more existential terms of biologist and student of science and society, Tom Stonier declares, "*Information exists*. It does not need to be perceived to exist. It does not need to be *understood* to exist. It requires no intelligence to interpret it. It does not have to have *meaning* to exist. It exists" (Stonier 1990, 21, emphasis in the original). Still, it is not necessary to accept Stonier's radical view for there to be important consequences for how anthropologists think about culture. As suggested above, such information models may help us avoid ingrained anthropocentrism and perhaps even biocentrism. Another key thing, I think, is to appreciate that information involves the processing of matter/energy, and this processing itself requires matter and energy.

In anthropology, the energy costs of culture (as information) and the evolution of civilization have been best elucidated in *The Eighth Day: Social Evolution as the Self-Organization of Energy*, a rather

neglected work by Richard Newbold Adams that is far less mechanistic than the out-of-date perspective on complexity given by Leslie
White. Here is a quote from a key passage:

> the things we call ideas are themselves equally
> materialistic in the sense of being information,
> variously, in a nervous system, on a sheet of paper,
> as dissipating sound waves, or in some other energy
> form. Just as information inevitably characterizes
> energy forms, so meanings and mental models are
> inevitable components of human nervous systems ...
> [plus] the association that a collectivity of nervous
> system activities has with other things. (Adams
> 1988, 88)

Obviously, this relates directly to the old issue in anthropology of
"materialist" versus "idealist" perspectives. Adams shows that this
dichotomy evaporates with a better understanding of the thermodynamics of semiotic processes. What I think this also calls to our
attention is the need for a more encompassing kind of semiotics than
is given in the usual Geertzian interpretive perspective—Gregory
Bateson (1979) understood this well. Those, in particular, who embrace semiotics in the sense of the triadic process described most
famously by C. S. Peirce have also been particularly open to these
possibilities. Of course, how broad a sweep this involves is subject
to much debate. Some maintain that semiosis requires the high intelligence of complex central nervous systems in interaction; others
maintain that all life is engaged in sign processes, processes called
biosemiosis (Sebeok 1991; Hoffmeyer 2008). The most radical view
is that there is *physiosemiosis* (Deely 2000, 1999), wherein all being
is involved in sign processes, and being itself is thought of in terms
of sign relations (Bains 2006). All these distinctions beg a further

question about what exactly is information *processing*. In information processing, it is widely held that what is required is not just signal providing inputs but means to store, record, and respond to them. Purpose (or meaning) and intentionality come into play here as well (Feldman 2007).

For those trying to develop a holistic way of understanding the biological, the psychological, and the social, unraveling the difficult relationship between meaning and information remains a most daunting problem. Some, like Aunger (2002), approach the problem by reconceptualizing mind and culture in terms of information replicators and what he labels "instigators," both of which have physical and organic correlates. First, he notes that certain kinds of biological structures are different from physical ones because of the way they channel and constrain possible signals through their structural configurations (Aungur 2002, 148). Second, with reference to how specific patterns of information (memes), located in brains, have social influence, he argues that our communications "are projected like arrows into the environment, with which they must interact (hence the confusion that they are themselves interactors). Signals then migrate through the macroenvironment to a novel host (gaining contact through some sensory organ) and are translated back into neural impulses. Once within the brain, they are passed through neural connections to a location where they give birth to a new meme by stimulating a node in the new network, leaving it in a memetic state" (Aunger 2002, 241). Deacon (2012, 372) develops a different biosemiotic perspective by emphasizing that "what matters in the case of information, and produces its distinctive physical consequences, is a relationship to something not there. Information is the archetypical absential concept." What he means by this is that it is not just gathering dark clouds in the sky that impel us to take cover but our understanding of what the clouds imply for our future. The information that is not there, that it is going to rain, is "abstential" but also full of referential significance. Further, Deacon argues that it is crucial to distinguish between three types of information that emerge one from the other: one, information relating to signal and channel; two, information concerning order and work capacity; and three, information with teleological usefulness (Deacon 2012: 414-420). His perspective is rich indeed, yet, unfortunately, does not even have the term *culture* in the index.

As Brasdefer reminds us in the third paper in this volume, many matters of scale and mappings are necessarily involved in our studies. In addition to fact that distinct forms information processing are occurring at different magnitudes and speeds in embodied beings, there are also vast networks by means of which they are integrated; these may be expected to increase their complexity synergistically. If what makes consciousness possible is a form of "integrated information" that is generated "by a complex of elements, above and beyond the information generated by its parts" (Tononi 2008, 216) then how much more complex is that aspect of consciousness interlinked in social networks with others. The innovative and thought-provoking features of the works of Aunger and Deacon with respect to information suggest that there remain many potential avenues for new explorations in applying culture-as-information in anthropological contexts.

SOME IMPLICATIONS

Let me finish with discussion of a few implications. One is about the permeability of information environments, another about the nature of artifacts, a third about mappings and transformations of information in mind and culture.

From a biosemiotic perspective, information is exchanged wherever and whenever there is co-presence. This is because people have evolved to pay attention to other people, remember their interaction patterns for future reference, and make purposive typifications about them. More expansively, from a more physiosemiotic perspective, this exchange goes beyond a recording of social interactions in the familiar forms of social intelligence. A Spanish conquistador in the New World was necessarily a new type of Spaniard from the one at home not only because he was surrounded by new types of people. He was also different in that he related to a new realm of information that included a different geology, climate, ecology, and built environment. (One might also say the same thing about bonobos who have gone from the Congo to life in a zoo.)

Fieldworkers in cultural anthropology invariably impose barriers between themselves and their informants in that they seek time to rest or reflect, or that they try to limit the spatial and temporal domains in which information exchange occurs. Yet, you can't stop the flow of information. Even our material possessions "speak" about us in our absence—as many cultural anthropologists know from having their property examined and "interrogated" while they were absent from their research communities. Basic cross-cultural information exchange, which is often inadvertent and frequently erroneously interpreted, is exemplified nicely in Marjorie Shostak's description of the relationship between the !Kung and fieldworkers who preceded her in the Kalahari:

> The !Kung had been observing anthropologists for almost six years and had learned quite a bit about them. Precedents had been set that the !Kung expected us to follow. That was difficult, because we were critical of

> much that we saw: a separate elaborate anthropologists'
> camp, tobacco handouts, payment for labor and crafts
> in money, and occasional excursions by truck to the nut
> groves. Determined to do things our own way, we packed
> away our inherited tent and moved into a !Kung-style
> grass hut in a !Kung village. (1980, 26)

The !Kung were learning about anthropologists as people and as powerful others from the moment that the anthropologists set up camp, but the anthropologists could not see this, perhaps because they assumed cultures were bounded entities. To her credit, Shostak took stock of the situation quickly and moved almost immediately to establish co-presence with the !Kung on a more equal footing.

Shift frames now to archaeological considerations. What is an artifact in information terms? A standard dictionary definition is that an artifact is "any moveable object that has been used, modified or manufactured by humans" (Bahn 2004, 35). But we can also consider an artifact in terms of its information content and the traces of information it can provide to larger information complexes. Here I would distinguish between two levels of information that differ from Deacon's model in that they reveal how "aboutness" and "usefulness" are distinctly intermeshed in artifacts. (See Table 2.1.) While for modern humans, these levels are intertwined, it is useful to keep them analytically distinct for purposes of unraveling their significance in archaeological or primatological terms or when the context of their use is unknown or has gotten muddled. The distinction between Level One and Level Two is that Level One can be analyzed extensively without necessarily understanding

Hypothetical Individual Artifact

Information
Level One

Level 1A — "Congealed labor" of production and acquisition

Level 1B — Information (knowledge) necessary for
production, acquisition, and use

Level 1C — Context of use and association with related
phenomena

Information
Level Two

Level 2A — Metaphorical associations and entailments

Level 2B — Meta-information on artifact fitness

Table 2.1. The artifact in information terms

deeper levels of culture or meaning. While to unravel the information content inherent in an object at this level may take analysis of mechanics or sophisticated techniques from geology, chemistry, and physics, it does not require consideration of the specifics of any particular language, for example. Indeed, if chimpanzees produce artifacts, they will leave behind evidence of Level One-Three. Level Two, on the other hand, necessarily involves symbolic processes. As such, without additional information, what the particular artifacts meant to others may remain opaque to us as outsiders.

The finer level divisions within the levels may be characterized as follows. In level 1A the information is inherent in the object. To borrow a phrase from Karl Marx, there is inherent in an artifact the "congealed labor power" of its production. What this means is that the process of producing an artifact leaves physical traces of the labor. Level 1B is more encompassing in that it indicates the information required to acquire the artifact material, produce it in final form, and employ it in some manner. Often this entails life-course and/or socio-historical experience with the same or related forms. In the terms of assemblage theory, *artifacts* are objects that reflect their historical relations of exteriority as well as their inherent interior structures. Reflect here on two examples—an Olduwan pebble tool and a polished jadeite axe from the Neolithic. Even if we can determine nothing for certain about their higher levels of meaning, there is still information content given in the structure of the artifact material and the nature of its manufacture. It is because of this that we can say that an Olduwan pebble tool is less sophisticated than an Acheulian hand axe or that a jadeite axe must have had some symbolic value in that it was traded extensively from France across Britain and Scotland even though we know from studying its internal structure that it shatters easily and could therefore have had little use value.

Finally, let me reference my own work in the ninth paper of this volume concerning people watching bonobos at the zoo. First, take the situation I call Mirrored Behavioral Analogies, where it is hypothesized that a bonobo hug is processed in the brain as a human hug. If true, this suggests that the person's observation is processed as a map is to its territory, what Bateson (1979, 125) in information terms called *template coding*. A transformation is made from one to the other, but with considerable fidelity. This can occur so commonly because it is a fundamental cognitive process for processing information. (Level 1A above would also be an example of template coding.) Because a template coding process for mapping interactions in mammalian species seems so basic, I wonder to what extent it can be overridden or modified by human cultural frameworks that deny any animal-human connection, that define other animals as prey, or that generally promotes callous disregard toward others rather than observation-based empathy.

In the information terms of Bateson and Adams, even the apparently trivial act of children saying "ooo—ooo aaah aaah" when they see a monkey or ape is worthy of some analysis. Where actually does such an "ooo-oo aaah aaah" template come from, especially as it is generally not being taught in the immediate setting? It must be stored in the brains of the children, then evoked in their individual minds by the primate as a stimulus that is mapped erroneously, if understandably, onto a cognitive frame for expectations of chimpanzee behavior. As Adams (1988, 89) notes, "Information in culture is constantly reproduced between human nervous systems on the one hand and the extrasomatic forms on the other, a process that involves a constant introduction of error." The "ooo-oo aaah aaah" vocalization reflects a set of individually realized transforms of a cultural configuration.

CONCLUDING COMMENT

As I have argued elsewhere (Shanafelt 2009), anthropology's conception of itself in terms of holism could benefit greatly by being augmented with an emphasis on combined (or synergistic) effects. I think the same can be said for definitions that link together information and culture. Our self-definitions do not go far enough in meeting the goal of fostering a less anthropocentric approach to the discipline; fostering interdisciplinarity, and mitigating concerns about reification unless they consider cultural information as emerging synergistically from the interactions of physical, biochemical, and psychological forms. These forms are not simply built up like static strata that Richerson and Hanebrink critique but are, to use the terms of Gilles DeLeuze and Félix Guatarri, assemblages connected like rhizomes in space and time.

NOTES

1. Some of the ideas in this paper were first expressed in Shanafelt (1995).

2. In particular, they emphasize the value of the study of "Fischer Information." Fischer information is a measure of the relationship between what is known and the total actual amount of information contained in reality. As such, it is an estimate of the amount of information we have accessed from an information source. It also suggests that some information will always remain inaccessible.

REFERENCES

Adams, Richard N. 1988. *The Eighth Day: Social Evolution as the Self-Organization of Energy*. Austin: University of Texas Press.

Aunger, Robert. 2002. *The Electric Meme: A New Theory about How We Think*. New York: Free Press.

Bahn, Paul, ed. 2004. *Dictionary of Archaeology*. New York: Penguin.

Bains, Paul. 2006. *The Primacy of Semiosis: An Ontology of Relations*. Toronto: University of Toronto Press.

Baldwin, John R, Sandra L. Faulkner, Michael L. Hecht, and Sheryl L. Lindsley. 2006. *Redefining Culture: Perspectives Across the Disciplines*. Mahwah, NJ: Erlbaum.

Bateson, Gregory. 1979. *Mind and Nature: A Necessary Unity*. New York: Bantam Books.

Bohannan, Paul. 1973. "Rethinking Culture: A Project for Current Anthropologists." *Current Anthropology* 14(4), 357-372.

Bonner, John Tyler. 1980. *The Evolution of Culture in Animals*. Princeton: Princeton University Press.

Boyd, Robert and Peter J. Richerson. 1985. *Culture and the Evolutionary Process*. Chicago: University of Chicago Press.

Clarke, David. 1978. *Analytical Archaeology*. London: Metheun.

Deacon, Terrance. 2012. *Incomplete Nature: How Mind Emerged from Matter*. New York: Norton.

Deely, John. 2000. "The Green Book: The Impact of Semiotics on Philosophy." http://www.helsinki.fi/science/commens/papers/greenbook.pdf.

_____.1999. "Physiosemiosis and Semiotics." In *Semiotics 1998*, edited by C. W. Spinks and J. N. Deely. New York: Peter Lang.

Delanda, Manuel. 2006. *A New Philosophy of Society: Assemblage Theory and Social Complexity*. London: Continuum.

Durham, William H. 2002. "Cultural Variation in Time and Space: The Case for a Populational Theory of Culture." In *Anthropology Beyond Culture*, edited by R. G. Fox and Barbara J. King, 193-208. New York: Berg.

Durkheim, Emile. 1933. *The Division of Labor in Society*. NY: Free Press.

Feldman, Jerome A. 2007. *From Molecule to Language: A Neural Theory of Language*. Cambridge, MA: MIT Press.

Fox, Richard G. and Barbara J. King 2002. "Introduction: Beyond Culture Worry." In *Anthropology Beyond Culture*, edited by R. G. Fox and Barbara J. King, 1-22. NY: Berg.

Freilich, Morris, ed. 1989. *The Relevance of Culture*. New York: Greenwood.

Gamble, Clive. 1986. *The Paleolithic Settlement of Europe*. Cambridge: Cambridge University Press.

_____. 2007. *Origins and Revolutions: Human Identity in Earliest Prehistory*. Cambridge: Cambridge University Press.

Goodenough, Ward H. 1954. "Cultural Anthropology and Linguistics." In *Language in Culture and Society*, edited by D. Hymes, 36-39. New York: Harper and Row.

_____. 2003. "In Pursuit of Culture." *Annual Review of Anthropology*. 32(1), 1-12.

Hoffmeyer, Jesper. 1997. *Signs of Meaning in the Universe*. Indianapolis: Indiana University Press.

———. 2008. *A Legacy for Living Systems: Gregory Bateson as Precursor to Biosemiotics*. Berlin: Springer.

Keesing, Roger M. 1974. "Theories of Culture." *Annual Review of Anthropology* 3: 73-97.

Kroeber, Alfred L., and Clyde Kluckhohn. 1952. *Culture: A Critical Review of Concepts and Definitions*. Harvard University's Peabody Museum of American Archaeology and Ethnology Papers 47.

Laughlin, Charles D., and C. Jason Throop. 2006. "Cultural Neurophenomenology: Integrating Experience, Culture, and Reality through Fischer Information." *Culture and Psychology* 12(3): 305-337.

Quiatt, Duane, and Vernon Reynolds. 1993. *Primate Behavior: Information, Social Knowledge, and the Evolution of Culture*. Cambridge: Cambridge University Press.

Renfrew, Colin. 2007. *Prehistory: The Making of the Human Mind*. New York: Random House.

Richerson, Peter J., and Robert Boyd. 2006. *Not by Genes Alone: How Culture Transformed Human Evolution*. Chicago: University of Chicago Press.

Roberts, John M. 1964. "The Self-Management of Cultures." In *Explorations in Cultural Anthropology*, edited by Ward H. Goodenough, 433-454. New York: McGraw-Hill.

———. 1987. "Within Culture Variation: A Retrospective Personal View." *American Behavioral Scientist* 31(2): 266-279.

Sebeok, Thomas A. 1991. *A Sign is Just a Sign*. Bloomington: Indiana Univerity Press.

Shanafelt, Robert. 1995. "Culture as Information: A Unifying Perspective?" *The Florida Anthropological Quarterly* 2(1): 20-33.

———. 2009. "A Wormhole to Kroeber's Whirlpool: Revisiting Cultural Configurations in Light of Complexity and Assemblage Theory." In *Histories of Anthropology*

Annual, Volume 5, edited by R. Darnell and F. W. Gleach, 52-76. Lincoln: University of Nebraska Press.

Shannon, Claude, and C. E. Weaver. 1949. *A Mathematical Theory of Communication*. Urbana: University of Illinois Press.

Shostak, Marjorie. 1980. *Nisa: The Life and Words of a !Kung Woman*. New York: Vintage Books.

Stonier, Tom. 1990. *Information and the Internal Structure of the Universe: An Exploration into Information Physics*. Berlin: Springer-Verlag.

Szilard, Leo. 1964 [1929]. "On the Decrease of Entropy in a Thermodynamic System by the Intervention of Intelligent Beings." *Behavioral Science* 9: 301-310.

Thornton, Robert. 1988. "Culture: A Contemporary Definition." In *South African Keywords: The Uses and Abuses of Political Concepts*, edited by E. Boonzaier and J. Sharp, 17-28. Cape Town: David Philip.

Tononi, Guilo. 2008. "Consciousness as Integrated Information: A Provisional Manifesto." *The Biological Bulletin* 215: 216–242.

Weiner, Norbert. 1948. *Cybernetics*. New York: Wiley and Sons.

Wright, Susan. 1998. "The Politicization of 'Culture.'" *Anthropology Today*. 14(1): 7-15.

Young, Paul. 1987. *The Nature of Information*. New York: Praeger.

Human Scales

Thomas Brasdefer

Though it is highly debated in contemporary social science, the concept of *scale* is far from alien to our everyday experience. From childhood we become familiar with a variety of scales and how to use them, be they the scales to which our model buildings and cars were manufactured, the scales we learned in school to gauge distance between two points on a map, or the scales we tried to overcome with our friends as we tried to establish the superiority of our garage band. Albeit less commonplace, our rapid evaluation of the seriousness and likely tragic consequences of earthquakes such as those that shook Haiti and Chile in early 2010 are made possible through the summoning of the Richter and Mercali scales as commonly employed in the media vernacular.

Ubiquitous as the term may be, we tend to overlook the connection between scale and reality—especially with the advent of technologies such as video games, Global Positioning Systems (GPS) and electronic media such as the Internet. When scale is computed automatically for us, we are left to wonder why we were ever using the cumbersome paper map, the messy glue and plastic model kit, or the large photocopied stack of flyers that had to be plastered around town. In any case, we rarely double-check that a model's dimensions correspond exactly to the original object or that the distance indicated on a map corresponds to that displayed on the odometer.

We know there is a scale, and we take for granted that it is correct. Similarly, when a *Los Angeles Times* headline states, "Chile's quake 500 times more powerful than Haiti's," (Wilkinson 2010) when the former was an 8.8 magnitude and the latter a 7.0 magnitude, we trust that the calculation is correct: even if further reading of the article actually refines the calculation to "512 times the shaking." We are certainly forgiving the approximation in the title on account of the extremely large multiplication we are being faced with and the sheer disquiet one can only feel about such destruction. In short, scales allow us to more tangibly experience objects at a distance. The loss in fidelity and minute differences are the price we are paying for having an understandable connection to this distance.

There are many reasons for scaling, first and foremost of which is consistency and accuracy of representation: model cars and airplanes are built to scale because we are interested in recreating the design of the life-sized object. From this perspective, there would be little or no interest in an absurdly misshapen model of an object. Maps would also be very frustrating if we had no point of reference in the landscape or in the map to use to gauge the places and distances we are trying to cover at a glance. By and large, it seems fair to say that scales are extremely practical instruments in their specialized applications, even though they are not entirely necessary to our daily lives. This could be said of most measurement systems because we often need to use arbitrary units in order to measure and comprehend the world around us. For instance, the same recipe may be expressed in metric or imperial units whether one is living in Europe or the United States. A lot of cooks, however, will not follow recipes by the letter (or indeed the numbers), and recipes will also use imprecise units such as "heaping teaspoons" and "pinches."

While it would be extremely practical to have a natural unit of measurement for every phenomenon that is the object of social

sciences, precise standards seldom apply to the study of human activities. This has led to the widespread use of *scale* in a variety of
loosely associated contexts. An illustration of this quandary has
appeared in the discussion on scale that has been agitating human
geography for the last twenty years: what started with the opposition of two camps analyzing the world in either economic or social
terms has culminated in recent research with attempts to eliminate
the use of *scales* altogether. *Scale* has, by and large, become a contested concept. Nonetheless, in my work on American Indian language
policies, I have found that scale may be the most appropriate concept
available to comprehend the intersection of government jurisdic-
tions in Indian country, especially with respect to language policy.

In this paper I seek to establish some guidelines for the use of scales
in social sciences. My thinking is inspired by both the disciplines of
geography and anthropology, related disciplines that seldom inform
one another. I believe that regardless of the object of study, a proper
understanding of how scaling works is necessary if we want to retain
our interest in generalization without ignoring investigation of the
unique. As such, American Indian languages present a very peculiar
case in history: indigenous peoples of the United States are constitu-
tionally the responsibility of the Federal government (Article I, Section 8), which has no authority on language policy (Amendment X).
As a result, the power of indigenous language policymaking should
belong to indigenous peoples. Nevertheless, since the 1831 Supreme
Court decision in *Cherokee Nation v. Georgia*, they have been judi-
cially considered to be "domestic dependent nations" and subject to
state law as soon as they step out of their reservations (and even more
so if they lose federal recognition). What I am interested in is how
the three levels of governmental authority are interacting, or in other
words, what the different scales of power correspond to.

I start this paper by tracing the history of the concept of scale with a focus on the particular input of political geographers. This discussion will serve as a stepping stone into the work of anthropologists who have tackled the issue of measuring human phenomena, with a special look at the approaches taken by linguistic anthropology. Finally I will provide my own vision of how scale can impact the lives of people with special respect to the languages of American Indian peoples in the United States.

SCALES OF HUMAN GEOGRAPHY

The different uses of the word *scale* mentioned in the introduction all pertain to a measurement system, a medium to visualize the extent of a concept. The term was used rather loosely until the second half of the twentieth century, as the amount of geographical material increased dramatically and prompted a debate on what exactly is meant by it. The discussion became more particularly ardent as social sciences turned more of their attention to the rise of international organizations and transnational exchanges.

Finding Scales

The first discussions involved two camps. One camp was lead by Peter Taylor (1982, 1988, 1994), a political and economic geographer who thought in terms of the units "world-economy," "nation-state," and "locality"; the second, by Neil Smith (1989, 1992, 1993) an anthrogeographer who was a proponent of "urban," "regional," "national," and "global" scales. While both systems divisions had the advantage of being both thematic and geographic, they very soon appeared to solidify in time and place ideas that could change in a heartbeat. These scales were nonetheless useful in terms of analysis: one phenomenon may be observable only on a local level, while others may unfold differently all over the globe. Many realized, though, that these scales in thinking may be imposing locality artificially in a world where a company with headquarters on one continent may own factories on one or more others, and distribute its products to people worldwide. As economic and human contact are changing, so is the role of government both in understanding and regulating these spaces.

Anthony Giddens has suggested that before the modern era, time and space used to be "embedded" in place: there was no technology standing between us and time or space, and we could only apprehend our surroundings based on our own direct perceptions (Giddens 1990). However, the introduction of written languages, maps, and modes of long distance transportation made "possible the substitutability of different spatial units" and allowed our place to be different from our visible and concrete space. This phenomenon, which Giddens called *distanciation* uses arbitrary referents that relate apparently distant elements. For instance, administrative divisions such as cities and countries are given a common identity by their location in a central organization (executive, legislative, and jurisdictional) whereas rural areas maintain their distinctiveness in that the people identify only with individual plots of land and core family units (Giddens 1981). Scales are one of these referents: they enable us to have an idea of the limits of our city or country without having to experience it firsthand. One of the characteristic features of the modern world that Giddens and others have identified is the pervasiveness of government in ordinary life, as well as the role government plays in the development of our "created environments" (Giddens 1984). This is certainly echoed in Michel Foucault's view of power and discipline: in order to ensure social control, governments have had to create their own technologies as the rapidly expanding size of populations and the sprawling of cities reached unmanageable extents (Foucault 1975). In other words, for governmental technologies to be efficient, popular definitions of families, estates, and cities do not matter as much as the space of government created by political leaders. These created environments, or *locales* as Giddens calls them, are containers in which power may be exercised; they may be of various shapes and sizes, from that of a household to that of a nation-state. It is notable that these locales exist and are recognized mostly by virtue of the authority given to governments and represent a mixture of landscape practicalities, landscape constraints, and power interests.

In the 1990s, the acceleration of globalization made it clear that a fixed scale could not contain the smallest local areas, let alone the larger world scale. Erik Swyngedouw (1997) argued, for example, that social sciences needed to conceptualize a "jumping of scales," the idea that scales could be related without being in direct juxtaposition. Swyngedouw noted for instance that an institution may develop strategies to cater both to local markets and follow international guidelines and still remain local. Such strategies effectively conflate the global and local scales into one new "glocal" scale. In his attempt to deconstruct the seemingly all-powerful concept of globalization, Swyngedouw further points out that due to popular and scientific use of the word *scale* researchers and end-users alike may have been misled into thinking of scales as congruent, impermeable units: "the scales are, of course, operating not hierarchically, but simultaneously, and the relationships between different scales are 'nested'" (1997, 169). Peter Taylor (2000) illustrated some awareness of this process when he laid a renewed emphasis on "world cities," cities that have gained more importance on the global scale than within the territory on which they are situated. As illustrated in modern economic crises, economies are so linked in complex networks and interdependent processes that one local phenomenon may be felt all around the world:

> To break free, we do not have to lessen our concern for states, but rather to see them as one important element in a nexus of power which straddles geographical scales. In fact, appreciation of the importance of interlocking scales is an important general mode of dismantling state-centric social sciences. (Taylor 2000, 28)

Arguably, this networking between scales could very well be a scale in and of itself: that of interconnectivity which would effectively negate the scales produced by associations of individuals. As a counterpart to this thinking, Sally Marston (2000) added that the influence of "patriarchy and the gendering of social relations of consumption and social reproduction" dismantled areal scales into observational units that need to take into account interpersonal relationships. In this view, spaces and places of our everyday experience are all relevant to scale, but they do not totally constitute it. Our challenge as researchers is thus to understand how a scale is formed—if only in discourse—and to clarify by whom and what it encompasses.

Refining scale

Lam and Quattrochi (1992) made important distinctions among three types of scales used in geographical study: (1) the *cartographic scale* connects elements on a map and elements in the lived world; (2) the *geographic scale* links all occurrences of one event into a coherent whole that can be isolated for study; finally, (3) the *operation scale* is how a scale plays out in action in the world. The cartographic scale is probably the most familiar example. It involves an absolute, numeral, measurement system as well as a relative measurement; it is supposed to be real-life represented on a map. Cartographic scales are the product of cartographers; geographic scales by geographers, and operational scales by operators (actors, agents). While the first two types of scales are important intellectually, they are the result of a choice, a mathematical and reasonable process. The operation scale conversely exists because of the agency and actions of society. Cartographic scales, once computed, are found in the key of our maps. Geographic scales, once our research agenda are set, can be found in our publications, the conventions we used in our work. Though we may be able to see what phenomena result from an operation scale, we may not know exactly where the scale begins or ends. David DeLaney and Helga Leitner noted this in their introduction to an issue of *Political Geography* especially devoted to discussing scale:

> The problematic of scale in this context arises from the difficulties of answering the question: once scale is constructed or produced, where in the world is it? Scale is not as easily objectified as two-dimensional territorial space, such as state borders. We cannot touch it or take a picture of it. (1997, 97)

In order to fathom their more intangible aspects, Kevin Cox (1998) introduced a new paradigm of scales that envisioned them in terms of their social construction rather than in terms of taken-for-granted assumptions about so-called reality. In this paradigm, geographic scales and operation scales are to be considered the product of a relationship between people and their surroundings. This is evident in what he calls *spaces of dependence* and *spaces of engagement*. Spaces of dependence are political boundaries, such as city limits, national borders, gated communities, which play an unavoidable role in organizing our experience even though they may represent apparently arbitrary fragmentations of space. Spaces of engagement inevitably happen when highly mobile human beings are interacting with the world. The space of engagement is formed by a networking of human groups and entities, which may belong to any of the traditionally accepted geographic scales, but also may intersect and transcend all these scales. With this perspective, Cox is calling geographers to "liberate [them]selves from an excessively areal approach to the question" of scale (1998, 21). A similar argument was submitted by Erik Swyngedouw, who pointed out that scales are often the result of a negotiation process rather than a definitive geographical reality:

> Geographical configurations as a set of interacting and nested scales (the 'gestalt of scale') become produced as temporary stand-offs in a perpetual transformative, and on occasion transgressive, social–spatial power struggle. These struggles change the importance and role of certain geographical scales, reassert the importance of others, and sometimes create entirely new significant scales, but—most importantly—these scale redefinitions alter and express changes in the geometry of social power by strengthening power and control by some while disempowering others. (1997, 169)

The manner in which scales of government are traditionally explained could not illustrate this argument more literally: each center of authority in the hierarchy has powers that extend only so far as inscribed in law. When fireworks are forbidden within city limits, there is a clear material end to the scale of a city ordinance. Nevertheless, it is not rare for individuals to transgress this scale on occasion and break the law: this is an operation scale in which fireworks are certainly happening, albeit illegally. This may happen at any time and in any space or place regardless of what existing scales of power are dictating. How can scales account scientifically for these moments that escape the traditional concepts of scale?

Undoing Scale

The most recognizable feature of scale is homogeneity: scales represent the interval between units of measurement. To continue the simile started in the introduction to this paper, there is no possibility of heaping scales or pinches of scales; they cannot be fragmented or distorted. Sallie Marston, John Paul Jones III, and Keith Woodward, have recently advocated a suppression of *scale* as a concept in favor of a flat ontology "composed of complex, emergent spatial relations." This is understandably an alternative to the pounding of scale into every researcher's shape of research:

> [I]t is necessary to invent—perhaps endlessly—new spatial concepts that linger upon the materialities and singularities of space. Manipulating a term from topology and physics, these consist of localized and non-localized event-relations productive of event-spaces that avoid the predetermination of hierarchies or boundlessness.... Instead, a flat ontology must be rich to the extent that it is capable of accounting for socio-spatiality as it occurs throughout the Earth without requiring prior, static conceptual categories. (Marston et al. 2005, 424-425)

Such a radical change has encountered a mixed reception: Arturo Escobar (2007) welcomed the initiative as a coherent effort within the trend in social sciences toward a "flattening" of social relationships. Conversely, Helga Leitner and Byron Miller (2007) refused to abandon scale, lest "we would be left with an impoverished understanding not only of the power relations that inhere in scale, but of the power relations that inhere in the intersections of diverse spatialities with scale." Marston, Jones and Woodward proposed that instead of *scale* the concept of *site* be used, symbolizing a more palpable geographical occurrence with all its uniqueness and complexities. Furthermore, their site does not predicate any form of intent, whereas we usually have to create scales, sites happen.

The debate on scale in geography is still ongoing and obviously extends far beyond the scope of the present paper. We can nonetheless add to this discussion the work of anthropologists who have had to transcend common areal considerations in order to pursue their research.

The Scale of Ethnography

As communication between separate parts of the world has become increasingly accessible, geographical, logistical, and ideological constraints that used to be considered barriers have lost their importance. Appreciation of this "globalization" has undoubtedly been a great catalyst for social scientists to re-envision scale and re-assess their disciplines. In recent decades, researchers in feminist studies, communication studies, and information sciences have realized that they must transcend established geographical borders (the spaces of dependence mentioned above) for empirical reasons more so than philosophical ones: power disputes and other issues of social justice do not only happen in tribunals and courts, they happen every day at every level of society (Featherstone 1990; Lash and Friedman 1992). Here, too, the attention of anthropologists has shifted from finding peculiarities in remote islands to understanding such global phenomena as the fast-spreading alienation of individuals in their own lands.

In the introduction to their volume on critical anthropology, Gupta and Ferguson (1997) described anthropological research in the late twentieth century: "The ground seems to be shifting beneath

our feet." This is to be taken literally and figuratively. Both the world
and their discipline were undergoing drastic changes, forcing eth-
nographers to review their assumptions and "try to find our feet in
a strange new world" (ibid.). Echoing this sentiment, Comaroff and
Comaroff called ethnography in the modern world working on an
"awkward scale" (2003). Somehow the tables turned, and anthropologists, who used to study the "exotic others," became faced with their
own exotic otherness. Nonetheless, their disquiet was not unique.
They were simply expressing the very same concern mentioned
above for geographers: for scale to be a valid scientific tool, it needs
to be able to account for "strange" and "awkward" moments in which
we find ourselves in the field. After all, what we commonly call our
field also has boundaries; these boundaries are set by our agendas,
our informants, and ourselves. If an archaeologist surveys a site to be
excavated in the landscape, what is the excavation site of the linguistic anthropologist? We cannot rope in all the speakers of a language,
or even a sample population, in order to study them.

The Locus of Language

Language is an essentially human attribute; it is produced spontaneously and cannot be delimited by traditional borders: speakers of
various languages are constantly crossing national boundaries, even
speaking languages that do not necessarily correspond with their
place in the world. How can language be constrained to a surveyable
area? Languages themselves are volatile, today more than ever, and
the speakers of languages are highly mobile. A surface enquiry of the
English language would yield a variety of English languages spoken
throughout the world. In terms of *scale* English is spoken virtually
everywhere, yet not everyone speaks the same English. Language
use was theorized using geographical terms relatively early in the

study of linguistics, following Saussure's distinction between *langue* and *parole*. Neustupný spoke of *Sprechbünde* in which speakers of different languages will understand one another, by opposition to *Sprachbünde,* which relates only to speakers of linguistically related languages (Neustupný 1978; Romaine 1994). Interestingly, the German term *Bund* is versatile, indicating either a geographical area or a societal bond: a *Sprechbund* is then a speech bond or a speech area, and a *Sprachbund* is a language bond or language area. Neustupný also noted that those two areas overlap but seldom coincide. Focusing more narrowly on the speakers, William Labov spoke of a "speech community":

> The speech community is not defined by any marked agreement in the use of language elements, so much as by participation in a set of shared norms. These norms may be observed in overt types of evaluative behavior, and by the uniformity of abstract patterns of variation which are invariant in respect to particular levels of usage. (1972, 120-121)

For Labov, the norms of a speech community are negotiated in each discursive situation and may be different from those they learned in school. A speech community therefore shares the linguistic "reference points" needed to achieve efficient communication: it is a site of linguistic exchange. It may be tempting to equate speech communities with geographical boundaries in the modernized nation-states, but the best efforts of some nations to remain linguistic monoliths are thwarted everyday by the simple act of communicating. Besides, if a nation were to disintegrate tomorrow, its language will still exist regardless of the new political boundaries. Nations, on the other hand, only seldom tolerate mixed allegiances.

Each utterance produces a new communication situation without necessarily annulling those that came before. The same applies
regardless of size considerations, be it a whole language or dialect
or code. This is why linguists have been fabricating their own tools
(such as the speech community) in order to define their field of study.
But the speech community itself remains imperfect, with many ways
to distinguish them (Gumperz 1962, 1982; Hymes 1972; Bucholtz,
Liang, and Sutton 1999; and countless others)."

There are times when languages/scales and their features become
organically enmeshed to create a new language/scale without there
being any centrally planned intention for it to happen. For instance,
there may be no linguistic reason to abandon a language, but there
are often ideological incentives to do so. This case is best exemplified
in colonial and postcolonial occupations, such as when the Spanish
colonized Jamaica. Having used military force to exterminate the
indigenous population, they all but eradicated the indigenous languages on the island. Several years later, when the British settled the
island with a slave population from Africa, they did not immediately
attempt to impose the English language, and the Jamaican Creole
was created, incorporating elements of the English language as well
as various African and indigenous influences. Creoles and pidgins,
born out of the very specific linguistic foundations of their speakers with substrates and superstrates of influences, are an embodiment of "scales" as they happen spontaneously and with little or no
codification.

In the "globalizing" world, speech communities have trans-
mogrified into entirely heterogeneous and dislocated communities
meeting in immaterial places such as Internet Relay Chat, Instant
Messaging or message boards. Such politico-cultural ventures as
La Francophonie also transcend place by bridging French-speaking
peoples across continents, while claims to autonomy from peoples in

Pays Basque, Sri Lanka, or Palestine are questioning the validity of seemingly well-established historical boundaries across the world. Going even further in deconstructing linguistic boundaries, Alessandro Duranti attempted to dismantle the terminology of *speech communities*. Since there is no foolproof way to find the boundaries of a speech community due to the mobility of speakers and the mutability of language, Duranti (1988) argues that speech communities defy quantification because they are above all "emergent and cooperatively achieved" (Duranti 1988). It is notable that these are the same qualifiers used by Marston et al. to describe their flat ontology (2005, *supra*).

Speech communities represent the extent to which languages are spoken, much as scale can be widely summarized as the extent to which actions may take place. However we name them, and I believe each domain has its own lexicon, the quantification of cooperative action is of utmost importance to social scientists who may want to accurately describe a nation, a football game, or an aboriginal tribe. This is more crucially true if we look down the line and consider how our research may be used to inform policies.

SCALE, LANGUAGE, AND THE CASE OF (AND FOR) AMERICAN INDIANS

The linguistic situation of the United States is very particular, with hundreds of indigenous languages still alive in spite of receiving no official recognition. The absence of linguistic provisions in the Constitution relinquishes language issues to the responsibility of individual states. As a result, some of them have enacted measures to establish English as their official and only language. However, Native American tribes have an established constitutional relationship with the federal government that is distinctive, and laws called Native

American Acts have been passed since the 1990s to protect their languages. One can see the potential areas of contention: Does the federal protection of indigenous languages interfere with state powers? Is the federal government allowed to pass language legislation when it applies to American Indians? If the latter were to pass their own legislation, would it interfere with both state and federal powers?

The very existence of indigenous peoples in the United States should be considered a challenge to traditional scales. Arguably, part of the specificity of the indigenous status is its recognition by the country in which they live, but one should not overlook the fact that indigeneity existed before said country even existed and thus has ideological roots just as much as modern national identities. In my view, scales exist before they are identified by researchers or the media; they are the result of prior organization. It has been pointed out before that the construction of scale is an eminently political process (Howitt 2003; Rankin 2003). Scales represent the actions of people with common interests, whether they be established by governments or industrial lobbies, flash mobs, or terrorist groups. Through their actions, they are looking to disrupt existing industrial, social, or geopolitical orders and activating a scale that was theretofore unrecognized.

Scale is evident not only in scientific discourse, but also in vernacular language. An example is the conceptualization of the landscape. In 2003, the *Squaw Peak* of Arizona Mountains was renamed Piestewa Peak in remembrance of the first US military woman killed in action and the first Native American soldier to die in Iraq. While the indigenous tribes of the area have another name for the peak, this change removed the offensive connotation of the former name. Those who choose to negate the indigenous frame of reference (or scale) may remain partisan to the name *Squaw Peak*, while those who recognize the importance of the indigenous scale in the area (and nationwide) will be able to respectfully use the name Piestewa Peak.

Nowadays, few people think of Native American tribes as centers of authority in the United States. Even though tribal self-determination has been an official policy since 1975 (P.L. 93-638), few advances have actually been made to recognize the political power of tribes (Castile 1998, 2006; Clarkin 2001). Steven Silvern, looking specifically at the treaty rights of the Wisconsin Ojibwe, argued that Native American tribes in the United States are a "third geographical scale" (Silvern 1999). This peculiar position is double-edged as it is generally afforded by the federal government who has the final authority and ultimately holds a large part of tribal monies and land in trust (463 U.S. 206). Every occasion for the tribes to define their own scale can be seen as an assertion of tribal power, lest the Federal government maintain a stronghold on tribal power based on habit alone (Morrill 1999). Until 1975, most tribes had to rely entirely on the Federal government if they wanted any change on their reservation, and even after the policy changed, the Bureau of Indian Affairs (BIA) was still reluctant to allow tribal power to be exercised (Deloria and Lytle 1984).

Even to this day, the US government has a crucial role in defining the indigenous scale, as only federally recognized tribes are allowed to exercise their right to self governance. Furthermore, even though tribes have the final decision on tribal membership, applicants need to receive approval from the BIA in the form of a Certificate of Degree of Indian Blood, which is based on tribal rolls that have historically been maintained by the Federal government (Thornton 1996). Language, on the other hand, cannot be determined by blood quantum. By enacting a language policy in favor of American Indian tribes, the US government has assumed its constitutional responsibility without encroaching on state rights. A proper understanding of the

American Indian policymaking scale informs us that its jurisdiction only extends so far as reservations do. Where does that leave the languages of non-recognized American Indian tribes? Since tribes with federal recognition are struggling to protect their own idioms, it seems unlikely that an unrecognized tribal group would find the resources to enact its own schooling programs, but they could certainly have an argument for their programs to receive governmental protection.

American tribes are often (re)presented in opposition to the modern world, the word *tribe* itself being still today associated with nearly pre-historical connotations. Quite to the contrary, I argue that in their quest to obtain their own set of laws and to build their identities from within the Western world American tribes set an example that should be followed by minorities and majorities alike.

CONCLUSION

There are many advantages to using scale in academic research: it is hermeneutically and heuristically useful, and it facilitates comprehension greatly for scholars and laymen alike. On a map, scale enables us to span the entirety of an area at a glance. In research, scale enables us to span the entirety of a phenomenon in one phrase. In many ways, research is often conducted on a certain scale, though it does not often bear this name. International cooperation has become a staple in our everyday lives, from manufacturing to telecommunicating, and the vocabulary of nations and boundaries is fast becoming obsolete. Scale allows us to recognize territories from their most tangible (cities, countries) to their most intangible (personal space, lands) applications. It drives us to take into account associations from their smallest (individuals, families, tribes) to their largest (pan-Africanism, pan-Arabism, pan-Americanism, pan-Indianism, social networks) extent.

In a modern world where distant locations are no longer synonymous with exotic others and where people living poles apart may have been raised in the same cultures, it is important to take into account both the location and the dislocations that are part and parcel of living in the contemporary world. The global scale is perhaps the best antidote to so-called globalization.

Much as *globalization* (or the scare thereof) has become a buzzword for policymakers and an excuse to erase local particularities and obfuscate regional differences, bringing in a multidimensional term such as *scale* values the local while still taking into account the global. Information Technologies use the term *scaling* to describe a system's ability to improve over time; scaling can only happen in a positive manner and what does not scale becomes obsolete. Unfortunately, it is more common nowadays to hear the expressions *scaling back* and *scaling down* in economics and finance, and the term has become laden with somewhat negative terms. In this sense, using Marston et al.'s concept of *site* may be a valid choice to avoid abuses of *scale* and lead to its expansion across the board of social science. I hope to have demonstrated that this is not an issue exclusive to geographers and that everyone will benefit from an improved taxonomy of human enterprises. It is urgent that we foster a link between the apparent homogenization thatv some people are striving to achieve and the deeper distanciations that result from fears of a totally uniform world.

REFERENCES

Bucholtz, M., A.C. Liang, and L. Sutton. 1999. *Reinventing Identities: The Gendered Self in Discourse*. Oxford: Oxford University Press.

Castile, G.P. 1998. *To Show Heart: Native American Self-Determination and Federal Indian Policy, 1960-1975*. Tucson: University of Arizona Press.

———. 2006. *Taking Charge: Native American Self-Determination and Federal Indian Policy, 1975-1993*. Tucson: University of Arizona Press.

Clarkin, T. 2001. *Federal Indian Policy in the Kennedy and Johnson Administrations, 1961-1969*. Albuquerque: University of New Mexico Press.

Comaroff, J., and John Comaroff. 2003. "Ethnography on an Awkward Scale: Postcolonial Anthropology and the Violence of Abstraction." *Ethnography* 4(2):147-179.

Cox, K. R. 1998. "Spaces of Dependence, Spaces of Engagement and the Politics of Scale, or: Looking for Local Politics." *Political Geography* 17(1):1-23.

DeLaney, D., and Helga Leitner, eds. 1997. "Special Issue: Political Geography of Scale." *Political Geography* 162 (February):93-97.

Deloria, V. Jr. and Clifford M. Lytle. 1984. *The Nations Within: The Past and Future of American Indian Sovereignty*. New York: Pantheon Books.

Duranti, A. 1988. "Ethnography of Speaking: Towards a Linguistics of the Praxis." In *Linguistics: The Cambridge Survey, vol. IV. Language: The Socio-cultural Context*, edited by F. J. Newmeyer. Cambridge: Cambridge University Press.

Eckert, P. 2000. *Language Variation as Social Practice*. Oxford: Blackwell.

Escobar, A. 2007. "Post-development as Concept and Social Practice." In *Exploring Post-development*, edited by Aram Ziai, 18-32. London: Zed Books.

Featherstone M. 1990. *Global Culture, Nationalism, Globalism, and Modernity*. London: Sage.

Foster, R. 2002. "Bargains with the Concept of Modernity." In *Critically Modern: Alternatives, Alternities, Anthropologies*, edited by Bruce M. Knauft, 57-81. Bloomington: Indiana University Press.

Foucault, M. 1975. *Discipline and Punish: the Birth of the Prison*. New York: Random House.

Giddens, A. 1981. *The Class Structure of the Advanced Societies*. Hutchinson University Library. London: Hutchinson.

———. 1984. *The Constitution of Society: Outline of the Theory of Structuration*. Berkeley: University of California Press.

———. 1990. *The Consequences of Modernity*. Cambridge: Polity.

Gumperz, J. 1962. "Types of Linguistic Communities." *Anthropological Linguistics* 4(1):28-40.

———. 1982. *Language and Social Identity*. Cambridge: Cambridge University Press.

Gupta, A., and James Ferguson. 1997. *Culture, Power, Place: Explorations in Critical Anthropology*. Durham, NC: Duke University Press.

Howitt, R. 2003. "Scale." In *A Companion to Political Geography*, edited by John Agnew, K. Mitchell, and G. Toal, 138-157. Oxford: Blackwell.

Hymes, D. 1972. "Models of the Interaction of Language and Social Life." In *Directions in Sociolinguistics: The Ethnography of Communication*, edited by John Gumperz and Dell Hymes, 35-71. Oxford: Blackwell.

Labov, W. 1972. *Sociolinguistic Patterns*. Philadelphia: University of Pennsylvania Press.

Lam, N., and Dale A. Quattrochi. 1992. "On the Issues of Scale, Resolution, and Fractal Analysis in the Mapping Sciences." *Professional Geographer* 44:88–98.

Lash, S. and J. Friedman, eds. 1992. *Modernity and Identity.* Oxford:
    Blackwell.

Leitner, H., and Byron Miller. 2007. "Scale and the Limitations of
    Ontological Debate: A Commentary on Marston, Jones and
    Woodward." *Transactions of the Institute of British
    Geographers* 32(1):116–125.

Marston, S.A., John Paul Jones III, and Keith Woodward. 2000. "The
    Social Construction of Scale." *Progress in Human Geography*
    18:33-38.

————. 2005. "Human Geography without Scale." *Transactions of
    the Institute of British Geographers* 30:416-432.

Morrill, R. 1999. "Inequalities of Power, Costs and Benefits across
    Geographic Scales: The Future Uses of the Hanford
    Reservation." *Political Geography* 18(1):1-23.

Neustupný, J.V. 1978. *Post-Structural Approaches to Language:
    Language Theory in a Japanese Context.* Tokyo: University of
    Tokyo Press.

Rankin, K. N. 2003. "Anthropologies and Geographies of
    Globalization." *Progress in Human Geography* 27:708–734.

Romaine, S. 1994. *Language in Society: An Introduction to
    Socio-linguistics.* Oxford: Oxford University Press.

Silvern, S. 1999. "Scales of Justice: Law, American Indian Treaty
    Rights and the Production of Scale." *Political Geography*
    18(1):639-668.

Smith, N. 1989. "The Region is Dead! Long Live the Region!"
    Political Geography 7(2):141-152.

————. 1992. "Geography, Difference and the Politics of Scale." In
    Postmodernism and the Social Sciences, edited by J. Doherty
    et al. 57-79. London: MacMillan.

————. 1993. "Homeless/Global: Scaling Places." In *Mapping the
    Futures: Local Cultures, Global Change*, edited by J. Bird et al.
    87-119. London: Routledge.

Swyngedouw, E. 1997. "Excluding the Other: The Production of Scale and Scaled Politics." In *Geographies of Economies,* edited by Roger Lee and Jane Wills, 167-76. London: Arnold.

Taylor, P. J. 1982. "A Materialist Framework for Political Geography." *Transactions of the Institute of British Geographers* 7:15-34.

————.1988. "World-Systems Analysis and Regional Geography." *Professional Geographer* 40(3):259-265.

————. 1994. "The State as a Container: Territoriality in the Modern World-System." *Progress in Human Geography* 18(2):151-162.

————. 2000. "World Cities and Territorial States Under Conditions of Contemporary Globalization." *Political Geography* 19(1):5-32.

Thornton, R. 1996. "Tribal Membership Requirements and the Demography of 'Old' and 'New' Native Americans." In *Changing Numbers, Changing Needs: American Indian Demography and Public Health*, edited by Gary D. Sandefur et al., 103-112. Washington, DC: National Academy Press.

Wilkinson, T. 2010. "Chili's Quake 500 Times more Powerful than Haiti's." *Los Angeles Times*, February 28. http://articles.latimes.com/2010/feb/28/world/la-fg-quake-not-haiti28-2010feb28.

Williams, C. 1988. *Language in Geographic Context*. Clevedon: Multilingual Matters.

PART II
Teaching and Practice

"I Didn't Evolve from No Monkey": Religious Narratives about Human Evolution in the US Southeast

H. Lyn White Miles and Christopher Marinello

OVERVIEW

Longitudinal data from a survey regarding beliefs about evolution and religion were taken from a 12-year sample of students enrolled in a general education introductory anthropology course at the University of Tennessee at Chattanooga from 1996-2007. The results show that 59 percent of the students accepted human evolution and combined scientific perspectives with Judeo-Christian religious views, spiritual or non-western views, or accepted evolution on its own. Student narrative explanations of their views showed evidence of William Perry's stages of college intellectual development. Fifty-two percent of the arguments gave internal justifications, while the remaining arguments were either ones from authority (e.g., "the Bible says...") or from evidence (e.g., "fossil evidence suggests..."). Ahistorical themes and misunderstandings about evolution, including that human history began with Jesus or that species are commonly created through hybridization, were frequent. College anthropology instruction should address these misunderstandings explicitly, utilize active learning assignments and critical thinking, and reframe the creationism-evolution controversy as a dispute among alternative religious views as a means to increase acceptance of human evolution and close the culture gap.

INTRODUCTION

The ancient Greek philosopher Thales of Miletus, in the sixth century BCE, was one of the first scholars to question religious and mythological explanations for phenomena and to advocate for examining natural causes (Thales of Miletus, unknown/1957, cited in Kirk 1957). Since the advent of the scientific method, societies have had to grapple with the gap between existing religious worldviews and received knowledge, and with new ways of knowing based on reason and empirical evidence with changing paradigms. The culture lag and insecurity in religious acceptance of many scientific ideas, including human evolution, has become even more challenging given the rapid pace of scientific discoveries and technological change. Major world religions, such as Catholicism, Buddhism, Judaism, Hinduism, and mainline Protestantism, have incorporated evolutionary theory into their belief systems, but the fastest growing religious groups, fundamentalist Protestantism and Islam, have still advocated literal biblical interpretations at odds with science and have been much slower to accept biological evolution, especially for humans (Armstrong 2001; Burton, Johnson, and Tamney 1989).

In fact, acceptance of evolution in the United States has declined from 45 percent in 1990 to only 40 percent in 2010, and the United States now ranks only 33rd out of 34 developed nations in acceptance of human evolution, placing it below both European and Asian nations and just above Turkey (Miller, Scott, and Okamoto 2007). Miller, Scott, and Okamoto (2006) found that fundamentalism in the United States was more aggressive and uncompromising than fundamentalism in Europe and Australia, citing that the rate of acceptance of evolution even by college students has declined to 55 percent, down 10 percent over the last 20 years. Studies of college science teaching also report considerable misunderstanding and extreme resistance of students to critical thinking about evolution (Dagher and BouJaoude 1997; Krammer, Durband, and Weinand 2009; Nelson 2007). Thus, our study sought to determine the acceptance of human evolution by a sample of Tennessee students, explore how students integrated evolution into their religious beliefs, examine their stages of intellectual development and misunderstandings about evolution, and formulate suggestions for teaching students whose beliefs are at odds with anthropological evidence.

METHODS

We surveyed students enrolled in social sciences courses from 1996 to 2010 in an ongoing longitudinal study of the integration of their religious beliefs and understanding of biological evolution. From a sample to date of 4,662 students, we selected a subsample of 846 students enrolled in Introduction to Anthropology during a 12-year period from 1996-2007. Introduction to Anthropology is a four-field general education course serving primarily freshmen and sophomore students at the University. The modal student in this course within the University of Tennessee system was a 19-year-old female who had taken one high school biology class with only a cursory treatment of evolutionary theory in earlier education (Krammer, Durband, and Weinand 2009).

Positions on Evolution

The survey instrument used in this study was based on positions on evolution adapted and modified from categories used by Eve and Harrold (1991), shown in table 1. Students reported demographic information, including age, sex, race/ethnicity, college year, major, and religion, and were asked to choose among five statements related to positions on evolution within a Judeo-Christian context: young earth creationism, old earth creationism, theistic evolution, spiritual and non-Western evolution, and natural evolution. This was followed by an open-ended request: "Please explain your choice below."

NATURAL EVOLUTION

I believe that the earth was formed billions of years ago, and that life evolved from exclusively natural processes, without divine intervention or a supernatural force. New species of plants, animals, and humans have evolved and have also become extinct.

SPIRITUAL AND NON-WESTERN EVOLUTION

I believe in a higher power, order, earth mother, forces, or spirits that created and/or is expressed through nature and the earth. The universe is billions of years old, and plants, animals and humans have all evolved from earlier life forms with many species becoming extinct. This spiritual force or power acts through nature.

THEISTIC JUDEO-CHRISTIAN EVOLUTION

I believe in God as a divine being that created and/or expresses itself through the universe. The universe is billions of years old, and plants, animals, and humans have all evolved from earlier life forms with many species becoming extinct. God has acted through natural forces.

OLD EARTH CREATIONISM

I believe in God who created the world more than 6,000 years ago, and perhaps even billions of years ago. Plants and animals have undergone changes through time; but humans have NOT evolved from earlier life forms and were separately specially created by God.

NATURAL EVOLUTION
I believe that the earth was formed billions of years ago, and that life evolved from exclusively natural processes, without divine intervention or a supernatural force. New species of plants, animals, and humans have evolved and have also become extinct.
YOUNG EARTH CREATIONISM
I believe in God who created the world in six literal 24-hour days, about 6,000 years ago. The species that God created have not changed AT ALL over time. Neither plants, animals, nor humans have evolved over time or become extinct. I do NOT accept human evolution.

Table 4.1. Five basic positions on the evolution-creationism continuum

Eve and Harrold (1991) defined young earth creationism as a traditional fundamentalist position based on literal interpretations of the Bible that the world is only about 6,000 years old and was created in six literal 24-hour days. The young earth position holds that species have not changed over time, resulting in no evolution of plants, animals, or humans. Old earth creationism is characteristic of conservative Protestantism and allows for a much older age for the universe, some change in varieties or species of plants and animals, but no evolution of humans—only special creation. Many, but not all, intelligent design proponents are old earth creationists in that they allow for long-term and universal evolutionary processes but view the resulting order and complexity as requiring an intentional and intelligent creator and supernatural specialness of the human species in the creator's image (Davis and Kenyon 1989). Theistic Judeo-Christian evolution combines both mainstream Judeo-Christian beliefs and an acceptance of the evolution of not only plants and animals, but also of humans. Spiritual evolution includes those who are more spiritual than religious, with beliefs in a higher power or meaning to the universe. It includes non-Western monotheists and polytheists, New Age, Native American, or spiritual paradigms based on nature. The natural evolution position is based exclusively on non-supernatural scientific principles and evidence of plant, animal, and human evolution. Natural evolution rejects religious interpretations, finds them irrelevant, or takes an atheistic or neutral agnostic position toward them.

The student narratives were compared with the position they chose and in the few cases they differed, primacy was given to the narrative explanation. The most conservative position on evolution was scored for students who chose options in between two positions, and their dual selection was noted.

Perry Stage of Intellectual Development

Of the 846 responses, 759 contained narrative explanations of student views. To evaluate the students' critical thinking, we used William Perry's (Perry 1970, 1981; Rapaport 1984) schema of four stages of intellectual development of college students: dualism, multiplicity, relativism, and commitment. Perry (1970) found that in the first year of college, dualistic students believed that there were absolute right and wrong answers and did not realize that knowledge was culturally constructed. Multiplicity developed by the sophomore year after students were exposed to a variety of conflicting viewpoints in college and were overwhelmed or confused by them. Students made a choice but did not reflect on or articulate their reasons. By the junior year, relativistic students matured, recognized the importance of context, and began to discriminate among the diversity of views to which they had been exposed to make explicit reasoned choices. By the senior year, many students reached the commitment stage and integrated their knowledge with their personal experience and identity, and were open to new responsibilities. These stages are not rigidly conceived. For example, millennial students now take longer than six years to complete college (Bowen, Chingos, and McPherson 2009), so there will be variation due to culture, region, context, and maturity level. However, Perry's schema is useful for understanding the progression of critical thinking as a measure of intellectual development and maturity.

The 759 narratives were also coded for type of argument, with 126 of the narratives containing multiple arguments, and thus, assigned multicodes. The student explanations of their views were coded as an argument from religious, scientific, or parental authorities, argument from empirical evidence, or argument from internal self-justification. Common themes or misunderstandings about evolution were also categorized.

Data Analysis

The data were analyzed using PASW Statistics 18 and Excel 2007. The qualitative narratives were analyzed by matching student statement to idealized content for each Perry stage or argument type and by identifying shared themes. Data derived from other courses from Spring 1996, Fall 1997, and Fall 1997 were used to develop internal consistency of coding by four raters, including the two co-authors and two student research assistants, and a reliability of 93 percent was obtained. We hypothesized that the majority of students would accept human evolution but that creationist students would be a significant subgroup within the sample. We hypothesized that most students would be in Perry dualism or multiplicity stages and that both evolutionist and non-evolutionist students would justify their views with external, especially religious, authority.

RESULTS

Perspective on Evolution

Figure 4.1 shows that about 59 percent (499/846) of students chose theistic, spiritual, or natural evolution and were able to combine evolution with their religious beliefs, if they had them. Students not accepting human evolution comprised 41 percent (347/846) of the sample.

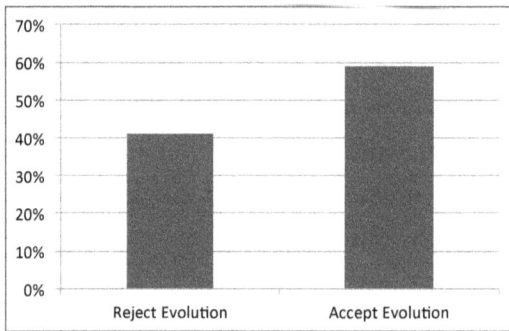

Figure 4.1. Perspective on evolution

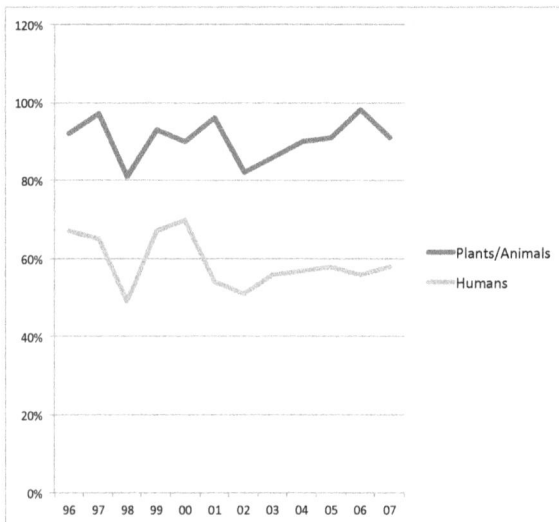

Figure 4.2. Degree of acceptance of plant, animal, and human evolution

Figure 4.2 shows that about 92 percent of students accepted plant and animal evolution or change within species, with a slight increase over time but that the acceptance of human evolution actually declined from 67.35 percent in 1996 to 58.17 percent by 2007.

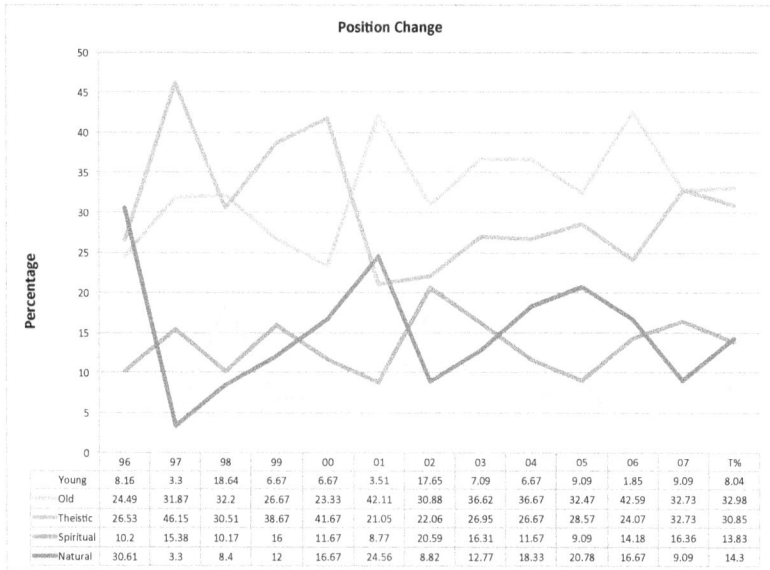

	96	97	98	99	00	01	02	03	04	05	06	07	T%
Young	8.16	3.3	18.64	6.67	6.67	3.51	17.65	7.09	6.67	9.09	1.85	9.09	8.04
Old	24.49	31.87	32.2	26.67	23.33	42.11	30.88	36.62	36.67	32.47	42.59	32.73	32.98
Theistic	26.53	46.15	30.51	38.67	41.67	21.05	22.06	26.95	26.67	28.57	24.07	32.73	30.85
Spiritual	10.2	15.38	10.17	16	11.67	8.77	20.59	16.31	11.67	9.09	14.18	16.36	13.83
Natural	30.61	3.3	8.4	12	16.67	24.56	8.82	12.77	18.33	20.78	16.67	9.09	14.3

Figure 4.3. Distribution of five positions on evolution: young earth creationism, old earth creationism, theistic evolution, spiritual evolution, and natural evolution

Figure 4.3 shows that the most frequent position selected by students was old earth creationism (32.98 percent), the belief in plant and animal change over billions of years with no human evolution. Theistic evolution was the second most frequent position at 30.85 percent; but when combined with spiritual evolution (13.83 percent) to show those who accept both religion and science, it is the largest group, at 44.68 percent. The two opposite extremes of young earth creationism and natural evolution were selected by only 8.04 percent and 14.30 percent of students, respectively. Over the 12-year period, old earth creationism and theistic evolution increased slightly from 24.5 percent to 33 percent and 26.6 percent to 30.9 percent, respectively, while natural evolution actually declined.

Stages of Intellectual Development

Of the 846 responses, 759, or 89.72 percent, had narratives explaining the student's choice that could be coded for Perry stages. (Some students chose a position but did not provide a narrative explanation.)

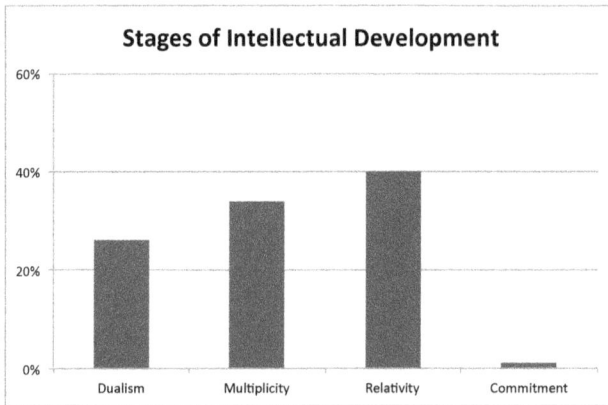

Figure 4.4. Distribution of Perry stages of intellectual development: dualism, multiplicity, relativism, and commitment

Figure 4.4 shows the distribution of the stages of intellectual development. Dualism was found in 25.69 percent of the narratives. Typical dualism statements are presented verbatim below:

Old Earth creationism

> I believe this because this idea is what I have been taught. The Bible that I read, King James version teaches me this. Starting in the book of Genesis where it tells that God created earth, man being (Adam) and from man a woman (Eve).

Theistic evolution

> I think that God did create the world long ago. He made us so that we will evolved throughout thing such as plants animals, and other living organisms. We will keep evolving until God tell us not to do so. This all God's plan.

Natural evolution

"Option 4 Big Bang Theory"

Multiplicity was represented in 33.73 percent of the explanations, in which students acknowledged at least two views and then made their choice with little or no explanation or expressed confusion or bewilderment:

Young Earth

> My opinion closely resembles options 1 [Young Earth] and 2 [Old Earth] because I believe that god did create the earth in 6 24-hour days. I believe that some species have evolved while others have stayed relatively the same.

Old Earth

> I don't know what to believe because I don't feel that I have seen accurate proof of any of this. I don't typically worry about how we came to be I just know that we are and someday I will know. If I don't—then so be it. The world is bigger than me and I have bigger things to worry about.

Interestingly, 39.92 percent of students gave evidence of Perry's relativism stage, the largest category, by making reasoned choices and explaining their viewpoints more completely:

Old Earth

> My religious beliefs are not clearly defined, but I think
> this idea is right. God being the creative force that started
> everything. One day in the creation = millions or billions
> of years in evolution. The whole creation story is the se-
> ries of events in chronological order. So basically they
> agree with each other.

As expected, commitment was a rare response, with less than 1
percent indicating integration of their views, identity, and their future career or personal commitment to others:

Spiritual Evolution

> Biology has long fascinated me, and evolutionary biology
> is no exception. I plan to attend graduate school study-
> ing zoology and/or evolution. As of now, I am a Meth-
> odist, but I wrote multi-denominational [on my survey]
> because I may start going to a different type of church…

Argument Type

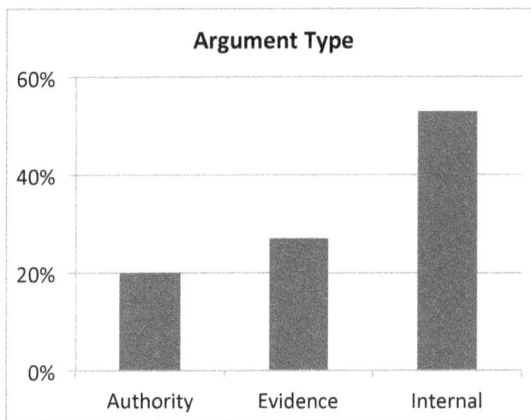

Figure 4.5. Distribution of Argument Types: Authority, Evidence, and Internal

Figure 4.5 shows that internal arguments were the most common, representing 52.99 percent of the narratives. Internal arguments showed the effects of enculturation and previous training, but
the students did not rest their primary justification on external authorities or evidence to draw their conclusions:

Natural Evolution

> To me there is no other logical explanation. I've tried in
> my life to get some sort of spiritual enlightenment, but
> it always seems to be questionable or too many grey ar-
> eas. Faith in god seems too faint to base one's entire life
> around.

Evidence arguments were the second most frequent, representing
27.23 percent of the narratives:

Old Earth

> I believe that humans have evolved mentally, more than
> physically. Fossil remains of earlier humans show differ-
> ent shaped skulls, but they are basically the same as ours
> today.

Natural Evolution

> Option 4 b/c with the presence of water and our so called
> bubble (ozone) around the earth makes our livable envi-
> ronment which can sustain life and we developed from
> micro-organisms to where we are today.

Surprisingly, external authority represented only 19.77 percent of
the explanations, the majority of which were made by young and old
earth creationists:

Young Earth

> "I have always been taught this throughout my entire life
> from both of my parents. Also I attend church on a regu-
> lar basis therefore it is a belief that is taught to me on a
> weekly basis." Another student explained, "I don't think
> humans came from no animals. That is none sense to me.
> God created Adam and Eve not a monkey or some other
> animal. If I agree with anything else I would strongly be
> going against my religion."

Narrative Themes

A strong theme present in the explanations was that college classes
should present both creationism and evolution together and allow
students to choose between them: "I hope that when we cover this
subject in class, it is covered equally on both sides. It would not be
fair to try to try to persuade students to one side or the other."

Many creationist students also were uncomfortable that evolution
regards humans as an animal species, and they sought to distance
humans from other animals as "special": "God created humans to be
Christ-like and animals to be just that. Nothing more. Nothing less.
No relation to me!!"

Students also showed a basic lack of understanding of the genetic
code and relatedness of species, seeing life forms as separate "types"
that shared no similarities. Students argued that for humans to share
the four-base pair genetic code with animals would be like being
"half-dogs": "He created after our seed so humans can't be half dogs
& half persons. An elm tree can be half elm and half apple. Cat is not
a half cat & half dog nor are any species that were created by God."

Both creationist and evolutionist students often thought incorrectly that species were commonly formed through hybridization,
including the human species: "I know that occasionally different

types of animals & plants will be bred together to create a slightly different plant or animal. How is this explained? Same with humans."

Many students saw most of creation, including plants and animals, as "old," while humans were regarded as "new" and special: "the discovery of fossils and other items ... have been proven to be over millions of years old. Man however I believe is special and has only inhabited this planet for about 6,000 years."

A number of natural evolution students mentioned that God had died or noted that God was merely an idea made up by humans for comfort: "God may have created the universe but if so He died in the process or has left it alone ever since." "I believe in God, but sometimes I find myself wondering what if we did evolve and there is no higher power. Sometimes I wonder if God is someone or something that we made up to motivate and give us hope." Some students were uneasy with the lack of absolute answers from science and longed for security and assurance: "The anthropology book said that science doesn't have a definite answer for everything and neither do Christians. But Christians can at least be sure of one thing ... God."

Especially disturbing was the surprisingly frequent claim that all of time and human history began 2,000 years ago with Jesus of Nazareth: "I really don't believe anything existed before Christ. I mean, come on, what was going on before then? Why would God make the Earth and wait billions of years to make people? He's not lazy." These statements did not seem to be metaphorical; they seemed to be meant literally.

DISCUSSION

Intellectual Development

The student narratives included earnest searches, humorous commentary, adamant religious statements, and involved scientific arguments. The large number of relativists among the students can be explained in part by the presence of some upper-class students in the course, but is more likely due to our instructions to the students to explain their position. If they complied, this immediately placed them in the relativism stage, greatly skewing our results. The fact that dualism and multiplicity narratives actually did not comply with our instructions and constituted 60 percent of the responses is the more salient finding. These nearly two-thirds of students gave flat one-sided statements or acknowledged the other side of the issue but made no attempt to relate their choices to their identity, major, or understanding of science or religion. There seemed to be two distinct groups of students: those whose worlds and experience were smaller and who focused on stable and secure received knowledge without much reflection or critical thinking and those who were more aware of context and evidence and less focused on absolute answers. These latter students were disproportionately found in the theistic, spiritual, or natural evolution categories. Internal arguments may also have been skewed because several students later commented that the survey made them worry that they would be chastised for their beliefs, which, of course, was not the case. It is possible that this artificially reduced the number of arguments from authority and increased the number from evidence and internal justification.

Most problematic was the theme in a number of the narratives that creationism and evolution should be taught as two alternatives to the human origins issue and that science could consist of supernatural explanations. The US National Academy of Sciences has stated that creationism and other supernatural perspectives are not science because they are not testable according to the scientific method (National Academy of Sciences and Institute of Medicine 2008). Nevertheless, creationism/evolution co-instruction has been desired by 56 percent to 80 percent of students from the 1980s to the present (Fuerst 1984; Krammer, Durband, and Weinand 2009;

Nelson 2007; Zimmerman 1986) in other student samples. This confirms that students feel forced to choose science or God, which can make preparation for social science or traditional college STEM careers in science, technology, engineering, or mathematics difficult.

Somewhat shocking was the number of students who dismissed prehistory and ancient history and questioned whether it existed at all. They argued that God would have only "wasted time" between the Big Bang and Jesus, and thus it "couldn't" have occurred. The notion that scientists and scholars would invent earlier periods of history shows the degree of disconnection with Western scholarship and intellectual discourse.

Teaching Human Evolution

The misunderstandings of students with poor science backgrounds or conflicting religious beliefs raises the issue of how to approach their instruction in an anthropology or other science class (Alters and Alters 2001; Brickhouse, et al. 2000; Loving and Foster 2000; Sinclair, Pendarvis, and Baldwin 1997). In this anthropology course, we explicitly discussed the intellectual stages and drew a parallel with how science works. We pointed out that scientists might start out thinking they are absolutely right (dualism), then become aware of alternative explanations or evidence (multiplicity), experience a paradigm shift (relativism), and finally develop an applied aspect (commitment). The Piltdown hoax, the shift from savanna to swamps in hominid evolution scenarios, or debate about DNA contributions of Neandertals are examples that show science changes as old ideas are discarded for new ones.

Second, we present the semester's survey results to students who are curious about where they stand compared with their classmates. This makes clear that there is great diversity in the class, and we stress that student positions might change as they learn more about evolution. It is important to make explicit that a college education, unlike high school, means that students engage with the material and see how knowledge has been culturally constructed. We stress that all religious views are respected but that students are learning the methods, theories, and values of anthropologists. At times, teaching these students seems like fieldwork, with culture shock and need for cultural relativism, because their worldviews are so dissimilar.

Third, we take a full lecture to review the history of how Western scholars came to distrust literal Biblical interpretations based on translations, copying errors, and contextual interpretations, at the same time that scientists determined the great age of the universe, saw that fossils were earlier lifeforms, and developed evolutionary theory to show the origin of new species. We model how science itself was in turmoil and had to adjust to the accumulation of evidence. We also present Web sites and documents of religions and their positions on evolution and how many have changed over time.

Fourth, research suggests that concrete experiential assignments rather than abstract lecturing is beneficial (Knapp and Thompson 1994; Nelson 2007). Gipps (1991) suggested hands-on fossil cast exercises to put the student into the role of scientist, and we use this and a number of active learning group assignments as well. For example, in one assignment, two panels of students confer with each other and physically arrange a group of fossil skull casts into lineages in chronological order. Then, we compare the two lineages and ask the evidential basis for the order and how the order would or would not be consistent with evolutionary theory. In another assignment, students form two chimpanzee or bonobo bands, create identities within the group; for example, dominant female, out-migrating sub-adult, tool innovator, etc., and demonstrate great ape cultural behaviors, such as termiting, nut cracking, medicine, political alliances, etc., to which they have been exposed in lectures, reading, and documentary films.

These exercises allow students to do anthropology at the same time that they create sensory empirical evidence, where students have had to reflect on ape-human similarites and fossil sequences.

Fifth, it is best to discuss misunderstandings about human evolution up front early on in a course (Skehan and Nelson 2001). Krammer, Durband, and Weinand (2009) identified five key misunderstandings as discussion points beginning with "science has proven that evolution is true" as a means to introduce the dynamic tentativeness of scientific theories. They next present evolution as a theory and creationism as a supernatural-based non-scientific approach, lacking falsifiability, testability, and the need for natural causation. Then they address the dichotomous thinking we also found in our sample, that if you believe in evolution you cannot believe in God. Last, they ask students to define evolution as a means to "out" all the misunderstandings. Krammer, Durband, and Weinand (2009, 27) found that seniors in college do not necessarily understand evolution better than freshmen and that "the basic foundations of science and evolution may not be communicated effectively and are not occupying a central role in some college-level ... courses."

Finally, enhancing overall critical thinking skills during the introductory course may be of ultimate benefit (Alters and Nelson 2002). Critical thinking is the process of conceptualizing and analyzing information with an eye to clarity, consistency, and depth and breadth of understanding, combined with an awareness of assumptions and cultural fictions, in order to evaluate various claims with a degree of confidence (Moore and Parker 2007). Many students come into class passively expecting only lecturing from an authority who will "teach the test" (Bowen, Chingos, and McPherson 2009; Meier and Wood 2004). Presenting repeated opportunities for active learning and discovery and doing critical thinking in all subfields of anthropology could generalize to more sophisticated means to engage with evolution.

Culture Lag and Acceptance of Evolution

Auguste Comte identified three stages in the social evolution of an idea (Lenzer 1997). A society first seeks theological religious explanations, followed by metaphysical and higher social concepts, and finally develops a scientific approach. Sociologist William Ogburn (1956, 1966) described culture lag as a maladjustment that occurs during periods of great cultural change. Woodward (1934) noted that symbolic culture lags most frequently behind material, scientific, and technological culture. Both pointed out that social conflict results if broad consensus is lacking, as we have seen in the recent court trials about human evolution in the schools. Closing of the gap may simply be due to later generations being born after the new discovery, so they take the new information for granted and integrate it into their worldview (Barnes 1974).

The gap created by the culture lag eventually closes, depending upon the degree of culture change and factors that might increase or slow its acceptance to the point that prior understandings now seem peculiar and unthinkable. For example, in 1835, two centuries after Galileo was tried for heresy and tortured for arguing that the earth revolved around the sun, the Church came to agree with the heliocentric view and began to honor Galileo for his achievement (McMullin 2005). After one Pope vilified Darwin (2009/1859) in the 1800s, in 1996, a hundred years later, Pope John Paul II (1997) finally accepted human evolution, declaring evolution to be not only a scientific fact but a discovery that aided Catholic religious understanding.

In the opinion of those who accept evolution, including many Christian clergy, the debate is no longer science versus religion but a conflict among alternative religious worldviews (National Academy of Sciences and Institute of Medicine 2008) that will take a number of generations to resolve. Our research shows that 59 percent, or slightly more than the average college acceptance of 56 percent, begin the course with no conflict with evolution. But what of the approximately 40 percent who disagree? The southeastern students in this pilot study who disagree do not have centuries to change—they have only a semester in which to adapt. Evolution is less extensively taught in southeast high schools than in the northeast (Krammer, Durband, and Weinand 2009; Lerner 2000; Moore 2001), and religious worldviews are often grounded in medieval thought. As a result, these students have only three months in a course to cover what took centuries to achieve. A deeper awareness of how they process and integrate scientific evidence about human evolution with their religion can help anthropologists understand how belief systems change and can assist anthropology programs to better formulate their instruction.

Still, the decline in the acceptance of evolution, and rise in court cases challenging it, is disturbing. The Scopes Monkey Trial in 1929 had a negative effect on science education (Eve and Harrold 1991; Larson 1997), and the recent 2002 Cobb County, Georgia, textbook sticker challenge and Dover Area School District (Pennsylvania) effort to introduce intelligent design as science has not helped (Petto 2005, 2008a, 2008c, 2008c). Some anti-evolutionary efforts are meeting with success; for example, the Louisiana Science Education Act 2008, which introduces creationism as a scientific alternative although it does not subscribe to scientific principles of falsifiability, replicability, and the evaluation of empirical evidence (Petto 2008b). But if anthropologists can combine experiential learning and excitement about empirical evidence with awe and wonder about the complexity of life, we may be able to reach out and move closer to closing the cultural science and religion gap for all students.

ACKNOWLEDGMENTS

We would like to thank Ralph Covino, Ph.D., Craig Nelson, Ph.D., and Shela Van Ness, Ph.D., for their comments on this research; Jessica Brand and Amanda Pippin for data analysis; and the UC Foundation for support of this research. The inspiration of Katharine Clemens, who served as a long-term mentor and friend who always encouraged the anthropological desire to see through cultural fictions, is gratefully acknowledged—she will be dearly missed.

REFERENCES

Alters, Brian, and Sandra Alters. 2001. *Defending Evolution: A Guide to the Evolution/Creation Controversy.* Sudbury, MA: Jones and Bartlett Publishers.

Alters, Brian, and Craig Nelson. 2002. "Perspective: Teaching Evolution in Higher Education." *Evolution* 56(10):1891-1901.

Armstrong, Karen. 2001. *The Battle for God: A History of Fundamentalism.* New York: Ballantine Books.

Barnes, Barry. 1974. *Scientific Knowledge and Sociological Theory.* Boston: Routledge and Kegan Paul.

Bowen, William, Matthew Chingos, and Michael McPherson. 2009. *Crossing the Finish Line: Completing College at America's Public Universities.* Princeton, NJ: Princeton University Press.

Brickhouse, N. W., Z. R. Dagher, W. J. Letts, and H. L. Shipman. 2000. "Diversity of Students' Views About Evidence, Theory, and the Interface Between Science and Religion in an Astronomy Course." *Journal of Research in Science Teaching* 37(4):340-362.

Burton, Ronald, Stephen Johnson, and Joseph Tamney. 1989.
    "Education and Fundamentalism." *Review of Religious
    Research* 30(4):344-359.

Dagher, Z. R., and S. BouJaoude. 1997. "Scientific Views and
    Religious Beliefs of College Students: The Case of Biological
    Evolution." *Journal of Research in Science Teaching* 34:429-
    445.

Darwin, Charles. [1859] 2009. *The Annotated Origin: A Facsimile of
    the First Edition of On the Origin of Species by Means of
    Natural Selection, or the Preservation of Favoured Races in
    the Struggle for Life*. Cambridge, MA: Harvard University
    Press.

Davis, Percival, and Dean H. Kenyon. 1989. *Of Pandas and People*.
    Mesquite, TX: Haughton Publishing Company.

Eve, Raymond, and Francis Harrold. 1991. *The Creationist
    Movement in Modern America*. Boston, MA: G. K. Hall.

Fuerst, P. A. 1984 "University Student Understanding of
    Evolutionary Biology's Place in the Creation/Evolution
    Controversy." *Ohio Journal of Science* 84(5):218-228

Gipps, John. 1991. "Skulls and Human Evolution: The Use of Casts
    of Anthropoid Skulls in Teaching Concepts of Human
    Evolution." *Journal of Biological Education* 25(4):283-290.

John Paul II. 1997. "Magisterium Is Concerned with Question of
    Evolution for It Involves Conception of Man: Pope John
    Paul II Message to Pontifical Academy of Sciences, 22
    October 1996." *Catholic Information Network*. http://www.
    cin.org/jp2evolu.html.

Knapp, P. A., and J. M. Thompson. 1994. "Lessons in Biogeography:
    Simulating Evolution Using Playing Cards." *Journal of
    Geography* 93:96-100.

Krammer, Andrew, Arthur Durband, and Daniel Weinand. 2009. "Teaching the 'E-Word' in Tennessee: Student Misconceptions and the Persistence of Anti-Evolutionary Ideas." *Reports of the National Center for Science Education* 29(2):18-28.

Larson, Edward. 1997. *Summer for the Gods: The Scopes Trial and America's Continuing Debate Over Science and Religion.* New York: Basic Books.

Lenzer, Gertrud, ed. 1997. *Auguste Comte and Positivism: The Essential Writings.* New Brunswick, NJ: Transaction Publishers.

Lerner, L. S. 2000. "Evolution: How Does It Fare in State K-12 Science Standards?" *Reports of the National Center for Science Education* 20(4):44-46.

Loving, C. C., and A. Foster. 2000. "The Religion-in-the-Science-Classroom Issue: Seeking Graduate Student Conceptual Change." *Science Education* 84:445-468.

McMullin, Ernan, ed. 2005. *The Church and Galileo.* Notre Dame, IN: University of Notre Dame Press.

Meier, Deborah, and George Wood. 2004. *Many Children Left Behind: How the No Child Left Behind Act is Damaging Our Children and Our Schools.* Boston, MA: Beacon Press.

Miller, Jon, Eugenie Scott, and Shinji Okamoto. 2006. "Public Acceptance of Evolution." *Science* 313:765-766.

Moore, Brooke, and Richard Parker. 2007. *Critical Thinking.* Columbus, OH: McGraw-Hill.

Moore, R. 2001. "Teaching Evolution: Do State Standards Matter?" *Reports of the National Center for Science Education* 21(1-2):19-21.

National Academy of Sciences and Institute of Medicine. 2008. *Science, Evolution, and Creationism*. Washington, D.C.: National Academies Press.

Nelson, Craig. 2007. "Teaching Evolution Effectively: A Central Dilemma and Alternative Strategies." *McGill Journal of Education* 42(2):265-284.

Ogburn, William F. 1957. "Cultural Lag as Theory." *Sociology and Social Research* 41(3):167-174.

————. 1966. *Social Change: With Respect to Cultural and Original Nature*. Oxford, England: Delta Books.

Perry, William. 1970. *Forms of Intellectual and Ethical Development in College Years: A Scheme*. New York: Holt, Rinehart, and Winston.

————.1981. "Cognitive and Ethical Growth: The Making of Meaning." In *The Modern American College*, edited by Arthur W. Chickering, 76-116. San Francisco: Jossey-Bass.

Petto, Andrew. 2005. "Victory in Cobb County." *National Center for Science Education*, January 13. http://ncse.com/news/2005/01/victory-cobb-county-00590.

————. 2008a. "Intelligent Design on Trial: Kitzmiller v. Dover." *National Center for Science Education*, October 17. http://ncse.com/creationism/legal/intelligent-design-trial-kitzmiller-v-dover.

————. 2008b. "Louisiana Antievolution Law Draws Scrutiny." *National Center for Science Education* 29(6):18-22, 27-28.

————. 2008c. "A Settlement in Selman v. Cobb County." *National Center for Science Education* December 19, 2006. http://ncse.com/news/2006/12/settlementselman-v-cobb-county-00804.

Rapaport, William. 1984. "Critical Thinking and Cognitive Development." *Proceedings of the American Philosophical Association* 57:610-615.

Sinclair, A., M. P. Pendarvis, and B. Baldwin. 1997. "The Relationship Between College Zoology Students' Beliefs about Evolutionary Theory and Religion." *Journal of Research in Developmental Education* 30:118-125.

Skehan, James, and Craig Nelson. 2001. *The Creation Controversy and the Science Classroom.* Arlington, VA: National Science Teachers Association.

Thales of Miletus. Unknown/1957. "Fragment No. 91." In *The Presocratic Philosophers: A Critical History With a Selection of Texts*, 2nd ed., edited by G. S. Kirk, J. E. Raven, and M. Schofield, 76-99. Cambridge: Cambridge University Press.

Woodard, James W. 1934. "Critical Notes on the Culture Lag Concept." *Social Forces* 12(3):388-398.

Zimmerman, M. 1986. "The Evolution-Creation Controversy: Opinions from Students at a 'Liberal' Liberal Arts College." *Ohio Journal of Science* 86(4):134-139.

Enculturating Student Anthropologists Through Fieldwork in Fiji

Sharyn R. Jones, Loretta A. Cormier, Caitlin Aamodt, Jade Delisle, Anna McCown, Mallory Messersmith, and Megan Noojin

Our paper describes year-one results of an interdisciplinary field school funded by the National Science Foundation Research Experiences for Undergraduates (NSF-REU) Program through the University of Alabama at Birmingham. This NSF-REU Fiji is a multidisciplinary collaboration among anthropologists (archaeology, ethnography, linguistics), historical ecologists, and educators (science education) focused on the understanding and conservation of cultural resources and marine biological variation. Our project established an international REU site in the Fiji Islands. During two summers (2009-2010), 18 undergraduate students (nine each summer) engage in this interdisciplinary problem-based research (field school) that is expected to generate a model of long-term dynamics in marine biological communities, emphasizing interactions between humans and the environment.

The philosophy of the NSF-REU program is two-fold. An underlying premise is that the potential for undergraduates to make meaningful contributions to science is often underestimated. If students are given the opportunity to engage in faculty research programs and if they are mentored in the scientific method and communication of research to professional audiences, they are fully capable, even at the undergraduate level, of making significant contributions to scientific inquiry. A secondary aim of the NSF-REU program is to target highly qualified but underrepresented populations of students. The aims of this paper are threefold. First, we discuss the project aims and the pedagogy of the student-scholar model, whereby students are incorporated into faculty research, beginning at the undergraduate level. Second, we present the findings of independent student research associated with the field school. Third, we provide an evaluation of the field school and its plans for the future.

BACKGROUND

The NSF-REU program is designed to provide meaningful research experiences for undergraduates, who often do not have serious research opportunities until the graduate level. Numerous educational theories and pedagogies exist in the literature that call for enhancing the learning experiences of students in college and university settings (Chall 2000). Our NSF-REU program is modeled on MATRIX, an NSF-endorsed anthropology curriculum enhancement and evaluation program designed to make anthropological teaching relevant for the 21st century (MATRIX 2003). MATRIX employs seven principles that focus on knowledge, skills, and values that are applicable to teaching archaeology, and for our purposes, ethnography: (1) promoting stewardship of anthropological resources, (2) recognizing diverse interests in these records, (3) understanding the social relevance of anthropology, (4) making a commitment to professional ethics and values, (5) developing effectiveness in written and oral communication, (6) learning basic archaeological and ethnographic skills, and (7) developing real world problem-solving skills. One of the key advantages of using MATRIX is that it was developed specifically to address the educational needs of anthropology students and to make them more marketable to potential employers after they graduate. Eleven specialists in educational anthropology created

MATRIX, and currently, thirty anthropology programs have contributed teaching modules to the MATRIX interactive Web site.

The UAB NSF-REU also seeks to make the field experiences of undergraduate anthropology students more relevant to their educational programs and future careers. Many of our undergraduate (as well as graduate) students have participated in study-abroad programs, collaborated with faculty in research, or had independent experiences (e.g., Fulbright scholarships, Operation Cross-Roads Africa, and varied archaeological and ethnographic field schools). Currently, little opportunity exists for undergraduate students to meaningfully translate these experiences into productive products that can contribute to their educational goals and professional development, nor do such opportunities exist for our graduate students beyond the thesis. The problem was described aptly by the Boyer Commission on Educating Undergraduates in the Research University (1998, 6); they argue, "Many students graduate having accumulated whatever number of courses is required, but still lacking a coherent body of knowledge, or any inkling as to how one sort of information might relate to others."

A priority of the UAB NSF-REU Fiji program is to provide continuity between the summer fieldwork experience and the rest of each student's education. The faculty serve as "scholar-teachers," where students are mentored and actively participate in the process of scientific inquiry and ultimately give presentations to both academic and public audiences; this model has benefited students in terms of achievement and retention, as well as making students more attractive to future employers (Boyer 1998; E. Boyer 1990; Hu et al. 2008; USDE 2008). An explicit focus on critical thinking is a fundamental part of the field school, which numerous studies have described as being inadequately fostered in university classrooms (e.g., Boyer 1998; E. Boyer 1990; Chaffee 1988, 2004; Facione et al. 1995; Hu et al. 2008; USDE 2006).

Specifically, our NSF-REU is designed to accomplish four objectives: (1) to introduce undergraduates to the ways in which ecological, historical, economic, and cultural phenomena are connected; (2) to train students in research strategies that will identify and explore those connections; (3) to facilitate the in-depth involvement of students in original research that will contribute to the scientific understanding of historical ecology, biodiversity through time, and characterize the causes and rates of marine ecological change; and (4) to effectively measure the success of the project in achieving its goals, implementing curriculum, and facilitating learning. Our fourth goal is aimed at creating a model of innovative strategies for teaching field-based sciences and for evaluating the educational effectiveness of our approach. Our research program should also stimulate and encourage the REU students to pursue a graduate education.

This interdisciplinary project will contribute to the understanding and conservation of marine biological variation through two perspectives. The field school involves documentation of economically important extant marine faunas through ethnographic observations of modern marine exploitation patterns by local inhabitants in the study area on four diverse islands in the Lau Group (Eastern Fiji: Aiwa Levu and Aiwa Lailai, Nayau, Lakeba). These islands were chosen through Jones's previous research; their variability in size and physical structure is representative of the region's island structure, fauna, and varying degrees of human impacts. Second, we will generate retrospective data on marine diversity and exploitation through archaeological work (the bulk of our work in 2009). Together these data will characterize and clarify the causes and rates of ecological change in a representative insular marine setting. Both long-term temporal data and insights gained from Fijian traditional ecological knowledge (TEK) will facilitate the development of programs for sustainable use of marine resources in the study area and beyond.

STUDENT RESEARCH

UAB undergraduate and graduate students worked on five projects related to this broader NSF-REU program. Their research included work on ethnoarchaeology (McCown), marine resource exploitation and the relationship between biodiversity and climate change (Delisle and Noojin), archaeological investigations (Messersmith), and historical place names (Aamodt). The projects by McCown, Messersmith, and Aamodt were initiated during our fieldwork on Nayau and were part of each student's NSF-REU Fellowship research. Delisle and Noojin are both graduate students who began their laboratory-based projects using the material culture collected from excavations on Nayau.

McCown: Dumped, An Exploration of Material Culture of the Past and Present in Nayau, Fiji

McCown's investigation involved comparison of the composition of contemporary and prehistoric garbage sites in order to (1) assess changes in the composition of garbage over time and (2) to gain insight from the contemporary dump site in interpreting site formation processes in the archaeological record. Nayau provides an ideal locale for comparing past and present garbage sites due to the relative continuity in types of subsistence practices over the last 2500-3000 years, its comparative isolation from more acculturated and Westernized Fijian islands, and its small population size (approximately 400 people) that makes such a project feasible.

While an extensive literature exists in archaeology on garbology (Rathje and Murphy 2001), very little has been done in this area in the Pacific. Most publications on contact and change in the Pacific focus on the exchange of religious ideas or prestige goods in the context of colonization (Worsley 1957; Schwartz 1976; Toren 1988; Thomas

1991; Kaplan 2004). Few studies (Leach 2003) examine change over time in the less exotic, but just as (if not more) informative everyday items that constitute most of the garbage produced by societies. Four key questions are relevant for this pilot project and future research in this area: (1) What types of information about the daily activities are ascertainable from an analysis of the byproducts of material culture (i.e., garbage)? (2) What types of changes in the byproducts of material culture are observable over time and space in Nayau? (3) Can analysis of garbage reveal evidence of changes in intensity of culture contact with the more Westernized main Fijian islands? (4) Can changes in the composition of garbage over time be used to predict trends in patterns of contact with Westernized islands and accumulation of Western material goods?

McCown and Aamodt collected data from an area of high trash concentration outside the village of Salia. McCown developed an artifact classification system that encompassed all material culture remnants recovered in both the contemporary site and the archaeological site. The key findings of the research are listed below.

First, items of Western material culture were present in the contemporary site that were not present in the archaeological site. While this suggests increased contact with Westernized groups and acquisition of items of their material culture, it is not inconsistent with Fijian culture to materially express wealth and prestige. In the past and present in Fiji, prestige is expressed through images of abundance (Jones 2009a, 34). Contemporary demonstrations of wealth on Nayau stem from these historical contexts, "to a lesser extent, [from] western ideas about wealth" (Jones 2009a, 32-33), as islanders value both indigenous and foreign material items. As islanders continue to value foreign goods, it is likely that their consumption of these items will increase over time as well.

Second, changes in the archaeological data analyzed suggest that the people of Nayau are experiencing recent changes in their diet as a result of access to Western products. Flour and other non-indigenous starches have become staples in the islanders' diet. Jones (2009a, 107) estimates that 70 to 80 percent of food daily consumed by the islanders are starches referred to as *ka kana dina*, or "true foods." She provides a list of these starches ordered by most frequent consumption and importance. Flour and rice, the only two nonindigenous items listed, appear fourth and sixth out of eight, respectively (Jones 2009a, 107). The incorporation of flour and rice into a once strictly indigenous category of food indicates a dietary change as a result of increased contact with Fiji's main islands, and this does not include other nonindigenous foods that have been added to the islanders' diet.

Third, changes in the islanders' culture can also be seen through further observation of modern imported items in the dump, including a videocassette tape and a compact disc (CD). These items reflect the recent changes in villagers' access to media. During Jones' (personal communication) research on Nayau, there were no televisions or videocassette recorders, although a few islanders had generators. Now, several households in Salia have televisions, VCRs, and DVD players. The grade school on the island is currently seeking a generator, and the village of *Liku* now has a community generator through which it distributes electricity to its inhabitants. This change in energy dependence has occurred very recently, within the last decade, and islanders continue to use more electricity with each passing year.

Rapid changes are taking place on Nayau and seem to suggest urgency in conducting fieldwork. Although different aspects of the islanders' culture are changing as a result of increased contact, these changes are not necessarily damaging the islanders' cultural integrity. Several researchers (Thomas 1991, 2; Toren 1988, 696, 712-715) have suggested that increasing dependence on "modern" items will not result in the loss of the Lauans' unique culture, but rather that these items "enhance existing social systems and are looked upon as a positive influence" (Jones 2009a, 30-31). It is expected that Nayau, like most of the more isolated cultures of the world, will continue to be increasingly drawn into the forces of globalization. However, the people of Nayau are not so much replicating Western models, but adopting novel items into their own cultural domain and altering their use and meaning to reflect Lauan lifeways.

A number of steps can be taken to continue future research in comparing past and present depositions of material culture on Nayau. First and foremost, a map should be created of the contemporary area of high trash concentration excavated in the summer of 2009. The map should also include spatial relationships between the garbage site and living spaces, working spaces, structures, and landscape features such as the bush and the ocean to make it relevant for comparison to archaeological sites (see Jones 2009a, 63; Schiffer 1972, 161-162; Toren 1988, 700-706). In addition, a map of the dump outside of the village of Salia could be used to provide a basis for comparison for other dump sites on the island of Nayau. Furthermore, mapping the dump outside of Salia would provide a basis for comparison for other dump sites on Nayau. Interestingly, neither of the other two villages on Nayau have a dump comparable in size to Salia's. It is possible that the reason Salia has such a large dump site is that, for a number of years, the village has been without a chief, who would coordinate community activities such as garbage disposal.

Second, further research would help clarify differences between the ideal and real in terms of what islanders say they throw away and what they actually do throw away. Rathje (2001, 67) states, "What people claim in interviews to have bought and consumed, to have eaten and drunk, to have recycled and thrown away, almost never corresponds directly or even very closely to the actual remnants of material culture in their [garbage]." By using matched studies that compare interview data with the cycle of contemporary material culture of the islanders from source to refuse, a more accurate picture of consumption of both indigenous and nonindigenous products would emerge. Jones (2009a, 110) notes that according to her interviews, frequency of store visits and sums of purchases made does not appear to be directly related to age or rank of the consumer, but rather to the amount of disposable cash available to the consumer. New interviews and descriptions of material culture could be matched one to one to demonstrate correlations between consumption patterns and age, gender, and social status. Jones and others accomplish this in relation to indigenous items; further research here would focus on the consumption and disposal of nonindigenous items according to social standing. Additional excavations of the dump have potential to provide quantitative data amenable to statistical analysis on the most prevalent nonindigenous items in the dump. This could be combined with studies on other methods of disposal on the island to determine the percentage of garbage that is dumped, burned, and reused in order to adequately assess the extent of the garbage problem on Nayau.

More broadly, Schiffer (1972, 163) argues that additional research should investigate the dumping patterns of both present and past cultural systems in order to further illuminate the types of information that can be gleaned from discarded material culture items, especially in regard to archaeological site formation. Following material culture from source to refuse in Nayau would provide a complete description of the use, meaning, cultural context, and ultimate deposit of material items in Nayau and would thus contribute to understanding how these different processes are expressed in prehistoric and historic sites. Further studies in the dump also have potential to

enhance understanding of demographic variables. Creating a cultur-
ally-specific formula to estimate population size from the quantity of
garbage produced would have multiple applications for archaeological interpretation (Schiffer 1972, 163; Rathje and Murphy 2001, 138-
150). Future garbage studies could examine environmental changes
through time in relation to human activity and material culture on
Nayau from initial settlement to present day in order to demonstrate
the impact humans have on the environment.

In conclusion, although this pilot study was limited in scope, the
comparison of an early occupation site and a contemporary garbage
site revealed clear differences in the types of material culture remains at the two sites. While the contemporary site, paired with ethnographic evidence, demonstrates increasing acquisition of Western
material goods, it does not necessarily mean that such goods are incorporated into the culture of Nayau in analogous ways, either materially, socially, or symbolically. Nonetheless, it is cause for concern
that the accumulation of Western garbage seen on Nayau includes
materials that are non-biodegradable or even toxic, such as old bat-
teries and plastic that unless physically removed off the island may
take thousands of years to degrade. Pursuing further research on the
contemporary material culture of Nayau would aid in refining the
classification system proposed here, make a complete assessment of
the garbage problem on Nayau, and also provide unique contributions to the theoretical realms of contact, change, site formation, and
globalization. It is hoped that the preliminary data described here
will form the basis for future research investigating how relationships of culture contact and culture change are reflected in trash.

Delisle: What Invertebrates Can Tell Us About Climate and Culture Change

In recent years, detailed and accurate ecological data has become available for the islands located in Remote Oceania, as defined by genetic and linguistic studies (Pawley and Green 1973; Blust 2008). The relatively slow development in this field of inquiry is partially due to the fact that Pacific archaeology is largely a post-World War II area of research. Moreover, it takes a substantial amount of time and effort to negotiate funding, conduct surveys, select excavation sites on islands that are often remote and difficult to travel to, and to train individuals in proper excavation techniques. Post-excavation laboratory analysis includes the time-consuming tasks of sorting, analyzing, cataloging, debating, and eventually publishing (Kirch and Kahn 2007). Much of Pacific archaeological and other historical scientific research in the region has used a model of Late Holocene climate change in the Central Pacific, based fundamentally on interpretations of data from other regions of the world, specifically continental Europe. Now researchers have come to understand that this Late Holocene climate change model conflicts with a vastly increased body of information now available about climate conditions specific to Oceania over the course of human history (Allen 2006; Field 2004). As a result, now more research can be conducted to generate informed conclusions about human history. The work described in this section details archaeological remains from the site and cave referred to by the Lauans on Nayau as Waituruturu. The goal of this project is to use archaeological data from Waituruturu's excavation unit J18 to explore the association between hypothesized climatic shifts and the abundance, size, and diversity of invertebrates through time.

Waituruturu ("falling water droplets" in Fijian, in reference to the moisture accumulating on the roof of the cave) is an archaeological site on the south side of Nayau. To get to the site, one must hike through the jungle for roughly one-and-a-half miles from the village of Salia, then uphill and over a number of prehistoric wall fortifications, to the entrance of a karst (calcified coral) cave covered in spongy green moss, ferns, and other vegetation. Evidence of former human and owl occupations is visible on the ground. Surface artifacts, including potsherds, shells, and bones are present on the bottom of the cave near the fern growth. Survey and excavations were conducted on this site in 2001 by Jones, and it was determined, through a combination of oral history and archaeological evidence, that the rock shelter was occupied during times of warfare and/or environmental changes that would have made it more difficult to survive on an island in the Central Pacific (Jones 2009a). Radiocarbon dating of archaeological remains indicates that the site was occupied briefly during the period of 680-520 BP (O'Day and Steadman 2003). The brief nature of the occupation during this interval, and the shifts in ceramic styles suggest that this may have been a time of social upheaval that was associated with ecological changes and cultural shifts that may involve contact from other groups of Pacific islanders (Jones 2009a). These movement patterns and cultural shifts might be related to the rapid cooling and sea-level fluctuations resulting from the transition from the Little Climatic Optimum to the Little Ice Age, which occurred between 730-525 BP, or around AD 1300 (Allen 2006; Jones 2009b).

With increasingly more detailed analysis, greater emphasis on data collection and preservation, and lively debate within academic spheres, the field of archaeology as a whole, and the archaeology of Remote Oceania specifically, has advanced a great deal in producing socially-relevant, question-raising, quality data (Kirch and Kahn

2007). In an attempt to continue this trend, Delisle conducted a zoo-archaeological analysis of invertebrates, specifically mollusks, from a unit excavated not far from Waituruturu's entrance. Though there were other fauna present in the unit, invertebrates were chosen as a subject of study, in part because of their presence at many different kinds of archaeological sites and the well-researched body of literature that goes along with those sites and in part because the information that fluctuations in shell size, population numbers, and frequency of Mollusca species potentially can be used to clarify the nature of human-environmental interactions both geographically and temporally. In the published literature on Remote Oceania, invertebrate faunal assemblages have generally been analyzed less than vertebrate assemblages, although the recent past has seen in-depth studies carried out for sites in multiple island groups (Jones 2009a; Conte and Kirch 2004; Green and Weisler 2004; Amesbury 1999; Morrison and Cochrane 2008).

Even minor climate changes may have impacted populations, potentially driving collapses in humans and other species. Though many people assume that in the past climate was similar to today's climate, the body of evidence from the past decade strongly suggests that climate has been incredibly variable over the course of human history. It is not a great stretch of the imagination to suppose that ecological events have had a considerable hand in shaping the evolution of entire genera of plants and animals, though there is also a great deal of evidence that suggests that periods of intense ecological hardship force interesting adaptations in species that maintain continuity and diversity into the present day. Environmental changes can also usher in periods of great success for both humans and the species they exploit, and more and more archaeological discussion is focused on the bounty and stability found in some human-inhabited environments before the present day (Baisre 2010; Jones 2010). More recently, studies of anthropogenic climate change have made clear that there are unintended consequences to human use and manipulation of the environment that can be viewed in the archaeological record and across the world today, but development and implementation of creative management strategies has equipped humans across the planet with the ability to deal with unexpected natural disasters and has allowed us to responsibly exploit our environments (Molnar and Molnar 2000). Natural processes associated with sea-level change and climatic fluctuation, as well as cultural factors related to changes in settlement patterns and resource exploitation, should be taken into consideration, all the while keeping in mind that ecological changes can lead to negative effects on near-shore areas, with consequences for the people who rely on these environments for subsistence (Morrison and Cochrane 2008). This is true for both the past and the present.

Mollusks usually are the most abundant fauna in Fiji's archaeological sites, and of the mollusks, taxa from four classes are usually the most common. Two of these common taxa were present in unit J18 at Waituruturu: bivalves and gastropods. In archaeological sites, shells are often found in middens, a class of archaeological deposit formed of refuse from food preparation and consumption. The term *midden* is also used to describe large mounds of shells (with associated cultural debris) found at archaeological sites. Unit J18 appears to be a *lovo*, or earth-oven, which contained fire-cracked rock and a substantial amount of charcoal, bone, and shell. The conditions at the site suggest that it was not occupied for long stretches of time, so the remains present provide a snapshot of the diet of the people of Nayau during a short period of settlement in a fortified site. The majority of the shells in unit J18 are relatively common bivalves, primarily *Atactodia striata* (surf clam) and *Codakia spp.* (Lucine clam).

The relationship between the shells found at Waituruturu and the people who consumed them could be coincidental and insignificant to the greater narrative of Lauan history, or they could be indicative of a creative survival technique utilized by the people of Nayau during a period of ecological marginality. We hypothesize that the women and children probably collected the shellfish, though who consumed these food items and under what conditions is up for debate. As with all sites, the exact conditions that led to the present state of archaeological remains extracted from unit J18 are still unknown, although it appears that ecological changes may have created conditions that facilitated movement and social change, but not necessarily a shortage of invertebrates. The rich biodiversity of the region appears to have padded the instability created by the weather shifts, with species ready to take advantages of increased storminess and fresh water from rain to initiate their spawning cycles. We know much more now than we did just a few decades ago about ecological conditions over time in Nayau, and this increased understanding can be supplemented further by looking at the people living on the island today.

As far as the ability of Fijians to exploit their environments to collect food is concerned, ecological extinction caused by overfishing precedes all other pervasive human disturbance to coastal ecosystems, including pollution, degradation of water quality, and anthropogenic climate change (Jackson et al. 2001). Evidence indicates that this is a cycle humans have been perpetuating for quite some time, and the negative impacts are abundant and visible, so much so that in some areas, species of marine invertebrates were once so abundant as to pose hazards to navigation and are witnessed now only by massive garbage heaps of empty shells (ibid.). Nayau appears to have maintained a high level of biodiversity and related stability in the variability of human diet, even during periods of intense ecological change when human subsistence is considered in a long-term per-spective (Jones 2009b). The archaeological remains, and our partici-pant observations of living Fijians, show that the island produces everything needed for successful long-term human occupation. Un-like the people who left the remains excavated at Waituruturu, mod-ern Lauans rely more heavily on imported foods, such as flour, sugar, and canned fish.

Several tropical Pacific Island cultures invented and employed marine resource management measures centuries before the West did, and for a variety of reasons, including to prevent the unsustain-able harvesting of species that eventually leads to extinction. These strategies included limited entry, closed seasons, closed areas, size limits, and in some rare cases gear restrictions. Recently, some Fijian communities have experimented successfully with population man-agement of certain bivalves, making progress toward littoral stabil-ity and sustainable exploitation (Dalzell 1998). Small-scale impacts from overfishing and pollution cannot necessarily be fully managed locally, as thermal stress and coral bleaching are already changing the structure of reefs. Impacts of climate change may depend criti-cally on the extent to which a reef is already degraded. Restoring food webs and controlling nutrient runoff from agricultural lots to avoid bacterial blooms provides a first line of defense against the ecological impacts of climate change; however, slowing or revers-ing global warming trends is essential for the long-term health of all tropical coral reefs (Pandolfi et al. 2005). Post-Cyclone Thomas, and because of concerns raised by climate fluctuations and species extinction, management programs such as the one described above might become a reality in Nayau in the future.

By combining what we know about the ecology of today with in-formation about the environmental landscapes of the past, we can approach the future with a more complete understanding of human impacts, successful strategies of marine resource management, and conservation (Jones 2007). Though there is some comfort in the fact that policymakers are turning to science to answer questions of how communities should deal with climate challenges, scientific, quantified knowledge is only one step on the way to creating an effective risk-management process (Finucane 2009). The people of the Remote Oceania, like people in every area across the planet, hold diverse beliefs about climate change, its causes and affects, and their individual roles in a greater global community. Their dynamic social and ecological context effects the decisions they make regarding consumption and management practices, and to a large degree determines the extent to which people are aware of and able to respond effectively to climate fluctuations and other ecologically relevant processes. Researchers working in environments such as Nayau see the impacts that changes in the weather and reef health have on the humans living in that environment. Though it is difficult to effectively communicate the detail necessary for complete understanding, improved methods of communication, conservation, and collaboration must be explored in the future in order to help preserve an ecosystem and culture that have already survived so much.

Noojin: Changes in Marine Biodiversity at the Site of Na Masimasi?

The purpose of this research project was to investigate possible changes in marine biodiversity as a result of climate change during AD 1300 (around the transition from the Little Climatic Optimum to the Little Ice Age). Noojin included two lines of evidence as part of her investigation—marine fauna and secondary sources or published studies. The findings indicate that there were several different types of marine species in the archaeological excavation unit examined (unit P18, a 1x1 meter excavation pit) at the site of Na Masimasi, but the area is very small and specific and can only be one small piece of the puzzle as far as showing any changes caused by climate shift. The site of Na Masimasi Yavu is a large earthen mound that was used as a structural foundation for a house or other building. It is located on the south coast of Nayau, about half a kilometer (or 0.3 miles) from the modern shoreline, and therefore the occupation has ready access to the sea. Radiocarbon dates indicate that the site was occupied perhaps as early as AD 0 and then continuously or at intervals through around AD 1520.

In a literature review associated with this project, a common theme was found in the discussion of natural versus human interference with the Fijian environment, and with Pacific environments in general. The literature has been helpful in discussing the various ways in which climate change can be traced, especially in regard to marine biodiversity, as discussed in the section by Delisle above.

The original plan for this project was to examine shell remains, or invertebrates in a midden context, excavated from the site of Na Masimasi Yavu in order to begin a database that would later allow for comparison of marine fauna from this region. This comparison is helpful in that it contributes to a broad perspective of marine life, sustainability of food systems over the duration of human occupation of Nayau, and potential changes that occurred over time. Specifically we aim to understand if shifts in the use of marine invertebrates are evidenced, especially during the hypothesized climatic shift around AD 1300 in the central Pacific. This study will thus address the issue of climatic changes and their potential relation to marine-oriented food systems.

While examining the shell midden from unit P18, several different types of information were collected in order to understand what invertebrates, and shellfish specifically, were available on Nayau, as well as to discover any changes in the use or exploitation of marine fauna over time. Information collected included element identification (genus, species), length, width, weight, count (NISP), and modifications. Modifications include any obvious signs of change in the shells that were man-made in order to make tools, ornaments, jewelry, etc. Tool classification included certain bivalve shell species, such as clams, oysters, and mussels that are used for scraping, as evidenced by use-wear along the edge of the shell. Overall, the invertebrate count is around 700, the majority of which are gastropods and bivalves, along with a small number of crab.

Some challenges were encountered while examining the marine fauna. In particular, accurate identifications of the shells were difficult due to the fragmentary nature of most of the specimens. Moreover, while there are online databases and literature on the topic of marine invertebrate species in the Pacific, Fijian waters contain much biodiversity and many species that are not well-illustrated and described in accessible databases or books. The marine species that made up the majority of the shells in P18 are those from the Turbinidae family. The Turbinidae family consists of a range of small to relatively large gastropods, commonly referred to as turban snails. A large portion of the shell assemblage was unidentifiable, being too broken and fragmentary to accurately identify and catalog.

This research suggests that there were likely copious supplies of shellfish, which occurred in a wide variety and that were available to the people of Nayau throughout the occupation of Na Masimasi Yavu, including the time period around AD 1300. The data gathered does not show a change in preference for the Fijians, nor does it show any changes in size, odd modifications, or changes in majority of species found when compared with data from earlier research and published literature. The shell size of individual specimens does not appear to differ from data collected by other researchers; therefore, this study found drastic differences in shell species. It is difficult to tell a great deal about possible climate changes and their effects on the marine subsistence economy based on this research project alone. The data show availability of shells, use of shells, and modifications resulting from use-wear on two bivalves. However, problems with gaps in our understanding based on this research can be filled by more exploration and excavation in Fiji. So far, several sites have been excavated and hundreds of different marine species have been cataloged from both archaeological sites and modern ethnographic research. The research presented in this section represents a small fraction of what can be known about marine biodiversity through time on the island of Nayau. This research is helpful in that it has added to a large database of known species found in Fiji and the Pacific so that, ultimately, we may be able to understand potential changes and effects caused by climate shifts.

Messersmith: The Fijian Lovo

Food, cooking, and eating all play prominent and integral roles in modern Fijian society, especially in the more traditional Lau Island Group of Eastern Fiji. Toren (2007) notes that Fijian household meals define and reinforce notions of hierarchical kinship relations. One's place at the table reflects that person's status in the household and/ or community. In regard to food preparation, Jones (2009a) observes that a significant portion of daily activities in Lau is focused on obtaining and preparing food. Special occasions, such as weddings and funerals require feasts. Jones (ibid.) also notes that places and activities dealing with cooking are both social and highly gendered. Given the pervasive connections between foodways and important aspects of society, such as social hierarchy and gender, the study of Lauan history and archaeology is incomplete without analyses of social spaces and the material culture associated with cooking and eating.

Lauans utilize two primary techniques for cooking: boiling on a hearth and cooking in an earth oven (or *lovo*). This paper examines a combustion feature that was partially uncovered during excavation in 2009 at the site of Na Masimasi Yavu. Although we suspected that the feature comprised a *lovo*, there were certain anomalies in comparison with previous examples of excavated earth ovens on the island. In order to answer questions about the nature and use of this particular feature, this research project examines common criteria that constitute a *lovo* in Pacific archaeology and analyzes this particular feature in regard to the criteria. After the basic analysis, Messersmith examines evidence for possible uses of the feature, including ethnographic and archaeological data that may point to a ritualistic or ceremonial purpose.

In order to determine if the combustion feature in question was in fact a *lovo*, Messersmith first determined a set of criteria common to earth ovens in the region that could be used for diagnostic purposes. While no such standardized list exists in the literature, she found several features that are commonly mentioned in both archaeological and ethnographic sources. These criteria include scoop and roughly circular shape, ash and charcoal in the sediment (sometimes layered), abundance of fire-cracked rock (FCR), and copious amounts of bone, shell, and pottery fragments (Carson 2002; Jones 2009a, 2007; Pietrusewsky et al. 2007; Steadman, Anton, and Kirch 2000). It should be noted, however, that these are general and very broad criteria that may differ on a case-by-case basis. For example, certain attributes, such as size, contents, and use of individual ovens, varied greatly among the reports reviewed.

In addition to archaeological data, researchers in Oceania have the advantage of the availability of ethnographic data about earth oven construction and contents. Although some practices have evolved (such as placing modern rice sacks on top of the food before covering it with dirt), Lauans today likely construct earth ovens much as their ancestors did thousands of years ago. By observing modern practices regarding earth ovens, we can draw parallels between the past and present. This may allow us to form a clearer picture of the construction and use of earth ovens in Oceania's distant past.

The unit excavated and analyzed at Na Masimasi Yavu is unit N18. It is located in the center of a house mound (*yavu*) in the broad area of sand dunes along the south coast of Nayau referred to as Na Masimasi (described in more detail in the section by Aamodt). The unit is located directly south of a large coconut tree. Root intrusion from the tree, and to a lesser extent from a smaller tree just south of the unit, made excavation difficult. Two radiocarbon dates were obtained from shells recovered from different levels of the unit. A *Turbo setosus* (turban snail) shell from approximately 40 centimeters below the surface (cmbs) gave a date of AD 1210-1320. At approximately 70 cmbs, a *Turbo argyrostromus* shell yielded a date of AD 660-790. A human bone from 120 cmbs of another unit at the site was dated to approximately AD 0. Taken together, these dates illustrate continuous site use and/or occupation from AD 0, the time of construction, to around AD 1320 or later. These dates place the site in the late or post-Lapita phase at Na Masimasi, according to dates from previous excavations (Jones 2009a).

After reviewing the stratigraphy of the unit, we determined that there are two main layers: Layer I (the combustion feature) and Layer II (non-combustion feature). The combustion feature extends down to approximately 80 cmbs. In general, artifact counts show a distinct difference between Layer I and Layer II. Pottery and lithic fragments appear only in Layer I. Also, shell and fire-cracked rock are significantly more common in Layer I. However, there is relatively little difference in the number of animal bones recovered from each layer, in fact very few animal bones were recovered overall.

Layer I consists of four sediment layers with poorly defined borders. The topmost layer (IA), was composed of dark (Munsell color

10YR 1/1) medium coarse organic sandy silt. Copious rootlets were present, and the layer showed evidence of having been recently churned up, probably due to a combination of agriculture and modern livestock, such as pigs, roaming the area. Layer IB, the dominant soil type within the combustion feature, appeared virtually the same as IA but was not disturbed by modern farming practices. There was also extensive root intrusion in this layer. Layer IC was found around the greatest concentration of FCR in the profile walls. It consisted of the same medium coarse organic sandy silt as the previous two layers; however, it was mixed with ash and charcoal, which resulted in a lighter color (10YR 3/1). Layer ID reflected mixing between Layers I and II (10YR 4/2).

The shape of the combustion feature corresponds with the common scoop shape of Fijian earth ovens found in both modern villages and previously excavated sites in the region (Carson 2002; Jones and Quinn 2009; Jones, Steadman, and O'Day 2007). Although the entire feature was not excavated, it is likely that the stratigraphy reveals approximately half the diameter of the scoop shape. Therefore, the estimated diameter of the feature would be about 2 meters. While most modern earth ovens on Nayau are between 0.5 and 1 meter in diameter, larger ovens are common in contemporary villages for cooking cows or large amounts of bread for feasts associated with special occasions (Jones 2009a).

Pottery sherds were found solely within Layer I, the combustion feature. A total of 37 sherds were collected, with a combined weight of 95.8g. Table 2 shows the different attributes present on the recovered sherds. Of these, 23 sherds were decorated with a thin red clay slip that is characteristic of Lapita and post-Lapita ceramics (Kirch 1997, 120). The slip on some sherds was virtually intact, while others had deteriorated to show only a hint of the red color they once displayed. Two sherds displayed a tan color different from the red slip.

Ten sherds showed evidence of mat impressions. These impressions could be deliberate, as a form of decoration. However, it is possible the impressions were unintended results of the pots having been laid on woven mats prior to firing. Also present were brush strokes from application of the red slip to the fired pottery. Finally, eight of the recovered sherds showed evidence of darkened areas or smudging, a result of the pot being used for cooking directly on a fire.

Of the 15 lithic artifacts collected during excavation, eight were later determined to be FCR. The remaining artifacts are composed of chert and fine-grain basalt. Fine-grain basalt was often used for tools throughout the Pacific, and such tools were considered more prestigious than those made of coarser-grained basalt. There are four basalt fragments, which all appear to be fire-cracked debitage fragments. Three of the lithic fragments are chert. Probably local, the fragments range in color. One is pink, another yellow, and the largest contains bands of both colors. The largest fragment retains the roughness from the original outer surface of the rock. It also shows signs of use-wear at the sharper end.

A total of 71 bone fragments, with a combined weight of 3.4 g, were recovered from unit N18. Of these, 40 were found within the combustion feature (Layer I). The remaining 31 fragments were located in Layer II, the area directly surrounding the feature. The majority of the fragments were found at depths of 20-30 cmbs (15 fragments), 70-80 cmbs (10 fragments), 80-90 cmbs (13 fragments), and 90-100 cmbs (13 fragments). The range of 20-30 cmbs comprises the top of layer IB, while the lower three areas contain the bottom of the fire feature and the levels directly below it. Of the bone fragments recovered from Layer I, 24 showed evidence of burning. These fragments were located in the mid to upper ranges of the combustion feature.

Fifty-four of the bones from the unit, a vast majority of the fragments, were positively identified as fish representing seven unique taxonomic categories. Forty-one of the fish bone fragments could not be identified, due to lack of diagnostic features. Seven of the bone fragments from unit N18 were identified as *Rattus exulans* (the Polynesia rat, which was introduced at the time the island was originally colonized by humans). Another seven fragments were echinoid (sea urchin). Other fragments were identified as snake, frog, and lizard. One fragment was an unidentified reptile, and another could not be identified to any specific taxonomic category. (Dr. Jones made the bone identifications.)

A total of 1194 shells were recovered from the unit. They have a combined weight of 1278.1 g. Of these shells, 953 were located in Layer I, and 191 were located in Layer II. One hundred twenty-seven of the shells from Layer I were identified, counted, and weighed in the field. Due to travel constraints, these shells were left in Fiji. However, the information collected was added to the total counts for unit N18. Of the shells processed in the lab, 54 were undiagnostic fragments of gastropods, 17 were unidentifiable bivalve fragments, and 329 could not be identified at all. Overall, 21 taxonomic families of shell were represented in the sample. While *Turbo* fragments were the most common in number, *Strombidae* (small conch) shells were also copious and yielded the highest minimum number of individuals (MNI) for the unit. Several of the shells were water worn, and at least one, a fragment of *Tridacnidae* (Giant clam), appeared to have been heat-affected, possibly the result of the shell being modified for use as a tool. Using both total fragment count and MNI, *Mytilidae* (mussel), *Cypraea* (cowry), *Tellinidae* (clam), and *Neritidae* (nerite snail) were common.

Fire-cracked rock is copious throughout Layer I. The first 10 cm of excavation yielded 79 individual rocks of cobble and pebble size.

However, it should be noted that heat from the fire feature might have caused some rocks to split completely, altering the actual rock count. FCR is abundant in higher levels and decreases in number in lower levels; the last 10 cm of Layer I contained only 12 rocks. This is most likely due to the scoop shape of the feature, which resulted in narrower sections of the combustion feature in lower levels. FCR was common in all three of the feature's levels.

In comparison with the other four units excavated at Na Masimasi during the 2009 field season, unit N18 yielded significantly more FCR. Units L12 and I22 had the next highest concentrations of FCR, with total weights of 23.2kg and 22.2kg respectively. Unit N18 contained about twice as much FCR, with a total weight of 42.9kg. Our research team excavated a probable earth oven feature in unit J18 at the rockshelter site of Waituruturu (described above). This feature contained considerably more FCR than unit N18, with a total weight of 232.6kg. Also present in J18 were layers of ash and charcoal as well as copious amounts of animal bone, much of it burned.

Overall shape, stratigraphy, FCR count, and the presence of bone and pottery support classification of the feature in unit N18 as a *lovo*. However, this combustion feature is somewhat unique among earth ovens excavated in Nayau and the Lau Group in general. Comparatively, there are significantly fewer fragments of bone and pottery in or around the feature. While charcoal flecking was observed, it was not present in the amounts that would typically be indicative of repeated *lovo* use. Ashy sediment was also present, but there were no distinct layers of ash. In addition, borders of the feature were clearly defined. Everyday ovens were repeatedly dug out and refilled, which would lead to a less distinct transition from oven fill to surrounding sediment. Taken together, these signs point to an interpretation of occasional, rather than everyday, use.

During fieldwork in 2009, the chief of Narocivo (one of the three villages on Nayau) visited the site at Na Masimasi. Upon seeing the combustion feature in N18, the *Tui* Naro told Jones that it was an earth oven used for cooking humans. He said this was obvious due to its large size, central location on a *yavu*, and copious amounts of FCR. When we inquired about why no human bone was found in the unit, if this was an oven for cooking humans, the chief explained that there were no bones because the bodies would have been removed from the oven after cooking and taken elsewhere, where they would be dismembered and distributed to the community's warriors.

Although the combustion feature excavated at Na Masimasi contained some anomalies compared to earth oven features in the region, we believe the basic structure of the feature classifies it as a *lovo*. However, relatively small amounts of charcoal, ash, bone, and artifacts point to a purpose other than everyday use as a cooking feature. While none of the previously published accounts of sacred spaces and rituals directly fit the ethnographic and archaeological evidence from Na Masimasi, the broad trends and variations within those trends do not discount the possibility of a ritual, perhaps even cannibalistic, purpose for the *lovo* in unit N18.

Further investigation into ritual and ceremony, both contemporary and prehistoric, could add an ethnographic perspective to the archaeological record for this and similar features. More extensive research of known ritual sites in Oceania could also contribute to our understanding of this feature's use and purpose. Ideally, further work would include a field survey of other nearby islands, incorporating ethnographic accounts and oral histories of modern inhabitants, to locate any similar features. The unique nature of this feature makes it an important area of analysis, not only for the archaeology of Nayau, but also for the entire region.

Aamodt: Place Names in Fijian Culture

Aamodt investigated place-naming trends on Nayau. Place names can be a rich source of information for understanding symbolic meaning, history, and social identities, values, and norms for a culture. As Edward Sapir wrote in 1921, the relationship between language and environment is negotiated by human cognition and social life. Given that the people of Nayau have continually inhabited the same geographic area using a similar subsistence technology for approximately 3000 years, the place names have potential to give insight into long-standing cultural traditions in terms of ecological adaptation, social relations, and ideologies.

Twelve place names were analyzed by Aamodt during the 2009 field season. They included names of villages, rock shelters, sites of historical significance, and some places that were associated with local mythology and oral history. The method for interpretation of place names included interviews with Fijian informants, personal communications from the project P.I. (Jones), and ethnohistorical and language reference sources (Calvert and Williams 1858; Capell 1984; Geraghty 1983). Broadly, the place names fell into two main categories: geographical names and cultural names. However, geographical place names often went beyond simply describing the landscape feature and also included cultural information. Below is a description of the twelve place names and an evaluation of the validity of the meanings obtained, based on the strength of the sources. Each are ranked on a scale from 1 to 5, with 1 representing a low level of validity and 5 representing a high level of validity.

1. *Salia* (geographical): "small reef passage" (Geraghty 1983, 153). Salia, the main site of the fieldwork, is a village on the southeastern side of Nayau. This name was given in 1979 after Hurricane Meli destroyed the original village. True to its name, the reef passage is

treacherously small. When the students in the field school first arrived, the captain of the ship initially refused to enter the reef because of the dangerous passage. Because this toponym is corroborated by the geographical feature, the validity is ranked at 5.

2. *Devo* (geographical): the former name of Salia; literally, "a variety
of soft stone, soapstone" (Capell 1984, 50). Because the specific stone
could not be identified on Nayau, the validity is ranked at 2.

3. *Waituruturu* (geographical): "water drops" (Jones 2009a); the
name derives from *wai*, meaning "water, liquid of any kind" (Capell
1984, 277) and *turu* "to drip, drop, of liquids" (Capell 1984, 243). The
site is a fortified rock shelter. Often the word *wai* in a place name
refers to water as a resource, either drinking water or fishing waters
(ocean or river). However, this designation does not apply to *Waituruturu*, where the water supply is not currently enough to drink.
There is some fern growth in the center of the cave that suggests that
there may have been a garden once, but there is no conclusive data
yet. It is possible that it serves simply as a poetic description and
identifying feature of the place. The validity is ranked at 5.

4. *Korovatu* (geographical): *koro* "an eminence" or "a village" (Capell
1984, 101), and *vatu* "stone, rock" (Capell 1984, 257). *Korovatu* is a
rock shelter, so the name translates almost directly to what the place
is. The validity is ranked at 5.

5. *Narocivo* (geographical): *civo* "a sudden gust of wind from the
mountains" (Capell 1984, 34) or "down" (Geraghty 1983, 135). There
is only one mountain on Nayau, a collapsed volcanic cone in the center of the island. While it is possible that the name *Narocivo* refers to
a geological phenomenon, this also may not be the true meaning of
the name. In 1858 (Thomas and Calvert), missionaries in Lau wrote
that the word *vakacivo* refers to the tradition of saying a kind of toast

or a wish after swallowing kava. These words may be commonplace, humorous, or sentimental. Wishes might include joking references to cannibal practices ("a human ham!"), or trade-specific needs, such as a report from the reef for a fisherman. Most commonly, people called out for wealth by naming specific items, including materials such as whale's teeth or food items. Often the wishes were encoded in enigmatic phrasing (Calvert and Williams 1858, 114-115). *Vaka* is a prefix added to words to make them causatives (Capell 1984, 251). So loosely, *civo* may refer to a wish voiced around a kava bowl. This older word may hold clues to the true interpretation of *Narocivo*. The validity is ranked at 1; further investigation of both wind patterns on Nayau and the significance of *naro* are needed to construct a working hypothesis.

6. *Nukutuba* (geographical): The name of a rock shelter, *nuku* "sand" (Capell 1984, 156), *tuba* "outside, but limited in use" (Capell 1984, 240). As might be expected, sand is copious along the shores of Nayau, and it is not surprising that there might be a reference to it in a geographical name. The second part, however, rings untrue. A more likely alternative definition for the second part of the name might come from the word *katuba*, which is the Lauan word for "door." The validity is ranked at 2.

7. *Raviravi* (geographical): The name for a fishing spot, *ravi* "to lean" (Capell 1984, 171). The name of this place describes how the fish appear to lean close to the rocks (personal communication, Jones 2009). As such, the fish behavior encoded in the term *Raviravi* may assist fishers in strategies for catching them. It is worth noting that *Raviravi* may be unusual in being formed from a reduplicated verb. Few other reduplicated place names were identified from either informant interviews or a review of the literature. The validity is ranked at 5.

8. *Nayau* (cultural): possibly *na* (an article, "the"), and *yau* "goods, wealth, riches, possession" or "to go in great numbers" (Capell 1984, 289). While it is not uncommon to see the association of land with wealth; it is unclear at this point whether these translations are correct, and further research is needed. The level of validity is ranked at 2.

9. *Liku* (cultural): translates directly to "native Fijian female dress, consisting of a band of braided *vau* or *wā loa*, with a fringe up to ten inches long" (Capell 1984, 121). In pre-European Fiji, the *liku* was everyday wear for women. It seems unlikely that Lauans would name a place after a female-associated item of material culture, when every other place name referring to ancestor gods identified thus far has a male-associated name. We suspect that there is an alternative, perhaps archaic, meaning of this word. The level of validity is ranked at 1.

10. *Na Masimasi* (cultural): "Sir barkcloth" (Jones 2009a). This site is a coastal dune and the place where the first founding ancestors lived, according to local oral traditions; now the site is plated as a coconut grove. It is the same site that Jones details in her 2009 book, *Food and Gender in Fiji: Ethnoarchaeological Explorations*. According to Jones (2009a), radiocarbon dates demonstrate that it is the oldest site occupied by humans on the island of Nayau, at 2800-3000 BP. Reports from the highest-ranking people on the island relate that it is the place where the gods of origin (*kalou vu*) lived when they first settled the island. *Masi* means "barkcloth," and the word is also used in the title *Ramasi*, which translates to "Sir Cloth." Here, it refers to the founding ancestors. It is common throughout the Pacific for legends to deify the first inhabitants of an island. The name *NaMasimasi* makes this area of the land a "place of the gods," as is traditional in Lauan culture and myth (Jones 2009a, 41-42). The validity is ranked at 5.

11. *Dali wawa* (cultural): Means "twisted intestines" (Jones, personal communication). *Dali* means "rope" (Geraghty 1983, 86) and *wāwā* means "intestines" (Geraghty 1983, 375), hill fort. According to Jones' informants, this name was created during a time when there was warring between the villages, and the purpose was to inspire fear in their enemies by evoking imagery of viscerally brutal war tactics. The level of validity is rated at 5.

12. *Qara ni timoni* (cultural): interpreted by a local informant as "the devil's cave"; *qara* "a hole or cave" may be a play on words, as another meaning for *qara* is "to serve, minister, attend" (Capell 1984, 162). The meaning of *timoni* is "demon" or "devil" (Capell 1984, 321-322). In Fiji, the people believe that the old ancestor gods, commonly referred to as "devils," or *timoni*, are still present but less effective than they once were, due to the fact that the people on Nayau now only serve the Christian God. This place name refers to a cave site where some people still practice rituals of the old religion honoring the old gods. Therefore, this name is a more recently conferred, post-Christianization. *Qara* may have a double meaning then, both "cave" and "to minister or serve." According to Calvert and Williams, Fijians do indeed enjoy punning, or *vakaribamalamala*. The example provided is a story of how the people of Mbau ordered the people of Tailevu to come to *ulaula*. *Ulaula* means both "to thatch a house" and "to throw *ulas*" (short war clubs). The people of Tailevu came expecting to help thatch a house but, upon arrival, were comically pelted with clubs. (Calvert and Williams 1858, 130). It is conceivable that the practice of *vakaribamalamala*, or a similar practice of play on words, is extended to the naming of places. The level of validity for the interpretation of this name as "the devil's cave" is a 5. The certainty of it having a double meaning is ranked at 5.

The examples above clearly show that place names serve several important functions in Lauan culture. Geographical place names that describe the features of the landscape have a practical function as orientation points in the landscape. They also encode information about the environment. For example, the term *Salia* provides valuable ecological information so that anyone coming to the village will know that the passage through the reef is very small. In a subsistence-based community, intimate knowledge of the environment is essential for survival. The Fijians have many epistemological practices to transmit this information, place names being one practical means of doing so.

Cultural names are a bit more abstract, but they also serve specific purposes within Lauan culture. One important purpose is to encode the history of the people of the island, such as with *Na Masimasi*. Retelling the history or mythology of places such as *Na Masimasi* also transmits values from generation to generation and recreates social and cultural identities associated with place. In more recent times, a similar function is seen in encoding information about current practices, such as with *Qara ni timoni*. Here the name may serve as a warning that the ancestor spirits present in the land have been recently attended to and may be more powerful than they usually are.

In sum, place names hold fascinating keys to understanding both present-day and past culture in Fiji. Many of the names in the study have definitive interpretations and associated meanings that provide ethnographic clues to the worldview and lifeways of the people of Lau. Other names require further investigation to truly understand what information is encoded in them. Plans for further study include reading more texts written by missionaries to find records of older traditions and words no longer in current use. In the field, additional research plans include having suggested interpretations evaluated by local informants, acquiring more place names and meanings,

mapping all names with GPS points and from there, using the map
to discern toponymic density, as well as utilizing records of indigenous oral history available in the archives of the Fiji Museum.

SUMMARY AND CONCLUSIONS

As the summaries of student research projects illustrate, our interdisciplinary program produced data that will contribute to a range
of important anthropological and biological issues. First, our archaeological data derived from the identification of animal bones and
shells is useful for understanding the potential impacts of hypothesized climatic shifts in the Central Pacific Islands at AD 1300 on
marine resources used for food. This long-term data on marine diversity and exploitation at the archaeological sites excavated in 2009
will be compared and contrasted to ethnographic data on important
modern marine faunas and contemporary exploitation patterns by
local inhabitants on Nayau (in particular, fishing and collecting on
the reef). Together these data will assist in characterizing and clari-
fying the causes and rates of ecological change in a marine setting.
Both long-term data (archaeological and ethnographic) and insights
gained from Fijian traditional ecological knowledge (TEK) will facilitate the development of programs for sustainable use of marine
resources in the study area and elsewhere. All of the NSF Fellows
were instructed in archaeological, ethnographic, and basic ecological techniques and gained skills and experience applying skill sets,
including mapping, excavation, sieving, documenting excavations
and drawing stratigraphy, interview techniques, note taking, jour-
naling, fish and shellfish identifications, and time allocation studies.

    Second, the exploration of material culture and refuse patterns
from an ethnoarchaeological perspective, the trash project, was designed to examine culture change and its material expressions. That

is, we aim to better understand material goods, their everyday use, value, and how they are disposed of. This work lends insights into long-term patterns of consumption and culture change.

Third, archaeological data from the site of Na Masimasi Yavu in particular provides information on ritual, ceremonial structures, and subsurface features (especially earth ovens or *lovo*). The oral histories and the material remains at this site suggest that this mound may have been used as a foundation for a temple or priest's house. The curious combustion feature in unit N18 and spatial, architectural, and artifactual analysis from the site as a whole promises to lend insights into the material correlates of ritual in Fiji, and in the Pacific Islands in general, a subject that has not been investigated in detail from an archaeological perspective in the region.

Fourth and finally, research on the place names of Nayau is informative and illuminates multiple dimensions of ideology in terms of symbolic meaning, social identities, history, values, and norms. The study of place names in Fiji is exciting, challenging, and rewarding, offering tangible connections to the larger understanding of worldview and indigenous traditional lifeways. It is hoped that in doing so, greater insight can be gained in seeing the land through the eyes of the Fijian people.

Some of the many accomplishments of our NSF-REU Fiji program have been described in the highlights above. In summary:

• Our 2009 team excavated two archaeological sites that will lend insights into long-term marine resource exploitation and ritual practices in the past.

• Students and program faculty collected ethnographic data (video, film, interviews) on traditional lifeways, eating behaviors, fishing, traditional ecological knowledge, changes in marine resource availability, body image, and ritual activities.

• Fiji Fellows designed and presented their findings and experiences to the general public and to local K-12 students in the Birmingham area (currently, a total of five days of presentations and 10 posters).

• The Fellows created an interactive website with the following address: http://hulamo.com/2009_NSF_REU_Fieldschool_in_Fiji.

• This NSF-REU Fiji program proved to be a challenging and beneficial learning experience. Most students described themselves as having a learning experience that will undoubtedly positively impact the course of their careers. Moreover, the changes in responses from the pre- to the post- experience educational evaluation tests clearly indicate large gains in both academic and cultural learning.

• Eleven professional papers were presented at regional and national professional conferences within the following year, based on data from this program.

• The Project faculty and students contributed to and/or authored both news items and lectures for students and the public in the Birmingham area and beyond.

In conclusion, relatively few opportunities are available for students to engage in meaningful research at the undergraduate level. While many anthropology field schools exist around the world where students and volunteers can gain hands-on experience doing archaeology or other forms of anthropology, a chance to engage in in-depth anthropological research in a remote setting with long-term cultural continuity is rare in our discipline. Our NSF-REU Fiji program trained students in participant observation and in conducting archaeological work and provided a setting where these skills were utilized in the field every day. For example, students learned to document fishing techniques, to identify common fishes, and to collect data from fishing expeditions, such as the species of fishes collected, their sizes and weights, the use of these fishes and how the members of the fishing party divide the catch. Upon their return from the fieldwork in Fiji, undergraduate and graduate students were trained in laboratory methods, and they gained experiences in a variety of outreach settings and media. Students worked to process, catalog, and analyze the artifacts and fauna. Students also created an interactive website that has background on the research project, a history of Fiji, information on our outreach program, podcasts with the fellows, a downloadable application to the field school, and contact information.

Student researchers gained experience presenting their findings and projects to the general public and to local K-12 students in the Birmingham area. While the presentations were educational experiences for the students, they were also educational for the general public and for K-12 school students. At the McWane Science Center in Birmingham, REU Fiji Fellows prepared four presentations and hands-on-science booths where people of all ages could learn about our Fiji research. Presentations and activities focused on the scientific method, archaeology, foodways in Fiji, and marine resource exploitation and management.

Our preliminary data analysis suggests that the field school was successful in meeting the educational goals set out for the students. Moreover, students learned and grew in ways that they had not expected. Most of them developed a sense of confidence and pride in completing the field school. The field school was undoubtedly transformative to all the REU Fellows and has stimulated positive associations with science for both undergraduates and students at the graduate level.

REFERENCES

Allen, M. S. 2006. "New Ideas about Late Holocene Climate Variability in the Central Pacific." *Current Anthropology* 47(3):521-535.

Amesbury, J. R. 1999. "Changes in Species Composition of Archaeological Marine Shell Assemblages in Guam." *Micronesia* 31(2):347-366.

Baisre, Julio. 2010. "Setting a Baseline for Caribbean Fisheries." *Journal of Island and Coastal Archaeology* 5(1):120-147.

Blust, R. 2008. "Remote Melanesia: One History or Two? An Addendum to Donohue and Denham." *Oceanic Linguistics* 47(2):445-459.

Boyer (Boyer Commission on Educating Undergraduates in the Research University). 1998. "Reinventing Undergraduate Education: a Blueprint for America's Research Universities." State University of New York at Stony Brook for the Carnegie Foundation for the Advancement of Teaching. http://dspace.sunyconnect.suny.edu/bitstream/1951/26012/1/Reinventing%20Undergraduate%20Education%20%28Boyer%20Report%20I%29.pdf.

Boyer, E. 1990. "Scholarship Reconsidered: Priorities for the Professoriate." Carnegie Foundation for the Advancement of Teaching, San Francisco.

Calvert, J., and T. Williams. 1858. *Fiji and the Fijians. George Stringer Rowe.* New York: D. Appleton and Company.

Capell, A. 1984. *A New Fijian Dictionary.* 2nd reprint. Suva, Fiji: Government Printer.

Carson, Mike T. 2002. "Ti Ovens in Polynesia: Ethnological and Archaeological Perspectives." *Journal of the Polynesian Society* 111(4):339-70.

Chaffee, John. 1988. "Teaching Critical Thinking across the Curriculum." Paper presented at the Annual Conference of the National Association for Developmental Education (12th, Orlando, FL, March 10-12, 1988). http://eric.ed.gov:80/ERICDocs/data/ericdocs2sql/content_storage_01/ 0000019b/80/1f/a0/ad.pdf.

———. 2004. *Critical Thinking, Thoughtful Writing: A Rhetoric with Readings.* 3rd ed. Florence, KY: Cengage Learning.

Chall, Jeanne S. 2000. *The Academic Achievement Challenge: What Really Works in the Classroom?* New York: Guilford Publications.

Conte, E., and P. V. Kirch, eds. 2004. "Archaeological Investigations in the Mangareva Islands, French Polynesia." Contributions of the Archaeological Research Facility, No. 62. University of California, Berkeley.

Dalzell, P. 1998. "The Role of Archaeological and Cultural-Historical Records in Long-range Coastal Fisheries Resources Management Strategies and Policies in the Pacific Islands." *Ocean and Coastal Management* 40:237-252.

Facione, P. A., Sánchez, C.A. (Giancarlo), N.C. Facione, and J. Gainen. 1995. "The Disposition Toward Critical Thinking." *Journal of General Education* 44(1) 1-25.

Field, J. S. 2004. "Environmental and Climatic Considerations: A Hypothesis for Conflict and the Emergence of Social Complexity in Fijian Prehistory." *Journal of Anthropological Archaeology* 23:79-99.

Finucane, M. L. 2009. "Why Science Alone Won't Solve the Climate Crisis: Managing Climate Risks in the Pacific." *Analysis from the East-West Center* 89:1-8.

Geraghty, P. 1983. "The History of the Fijian Languages." Special publication. *Oceanic Linguistics*. Honolulu: University of Hawaii Press.

Green, R., and M. Weisler. 2004. "Prehistoric Introduction and Extinction of Animals in Mangareva, Southeast Polynesia." *Archaeology in Oceania* 39(1):34-41.

Hu, Shouping, Kathyrine Scheuch, Robert Schwartz, Joy Gaston Gayles, and Shaoqing Li, eds. 2008. "Reinventing Undergraduate Education: Engaging Students in Research and Creative Activities." Special issue. *ASHE Higher Education Report* 33(4):1-103. http://www3.interscience. wiley.com/cgi-bin/fulltext/117902226/PDFSTART.

Jackson, J. B. C., M. X. Kirby, W. H. Berger, K. A. Bjorndal, L. W. Botsford, B. J. Bourque, R. H. Bradbury, R. Cooke, J. Erlandson, J. A. Estes, T. A. Hughes, S. Kidwell, C. B. Lange, H. S. Lenihan, J. M. Pandolfi, C. H. Peterson, R. S. Steneck, M. J. Tegner, and R. R. Warner. 2001. "Historical Overfishing and the Recent Collapse of Coastal Ecosystems." *Science* 293(5530): 629-638.

Jones, S. 2007. "Human Impacts on Ancient Marine Environments of Fiji's Lau Group: Current Ethnoarchaeological and Archaeological Research." *Journal of Island and Coastal Archaeology* 2(2):239-244.

————. 2009a. *Food and Gender in Fiji: Ethnoarchaeological Explorations*. Lanham: Lexington Books.

————. 2009b. "A Long-term Perspective on Biodiversity and Marine Resource Exploitation in Fiji's Lau Group." *Pacific Science* 63(4):617-648.

————. 2010. "Considerations for Advancing a Dialogue on Pre-modern Marine Exploitation in the Caribbean and Beyond: Comment on Julio Baisre's 'Setting a Baseline for Caribbean Fisheries.'" *Journal of Island and Coastal Archaeology* 5(1):159-161.

————, R. L. Quinn. 2009. "Prehistoric Fijian Diet and Subsistence: Integration of Faunal, Ethnographic, and Stable Isotopic Evidence from the Lau Island Group." *Journal of Archaeological Science* 36:2742-2754.

————, David W. Steadman, and Patrick M. O'Day. 2007. "Archaeological Investigations on the Small Islands of Aiwa Levu and Aiwa Lailai, Lau Group, Fiji." *Journal of Island and Coastal Archaeology* 2:72-98.

Kaplan, Martha. 2004. "Neither Traditional nor Foreign: Dialogs of Power and Agency in Fijian History." In *Cargo, Cult, and Culture Critique*, edited by Holger Jeebens. Honolulu: University of Hawaii Press.

Kirch, P. V., and J. G. Kahn. 2007. "Advances in Polynesian Prehistory: A Review and Assessment of the Past Decade (1993–2004)." *Journal of Archaeological Research* 15:191-238.

Kirch, Patrick Vinton. 1997. *The Lapita Peoples: Ancestors of the Oceanic World*. Cambridge: Blackwell Publishers.

Leach, Helen. 2003. "Did East Polynesians have a Concept of Luxury Foods?" *World Archaeology* 34(3):442-457.

"MATRIX: Making Archaeology Teaching Relevant in the XXI
    Century." 2003. http://www.indiana.edu/~arch/saa/matrix/
    homepage.html.

Molnar, S. and I. M. Molnar. 2000. *Environmental Change and
    Human Survival: Some Dimensions of Human Ecology.*
    Upper Saddle River NJ: Prentice Hall.

Morrison, A. E., and E. E. Cochrane. 2008. "Investigating Shellfish
    Deposition and Landscape History at the Natia Beach Site,
    Fiji." *Journal of Archaeological Science* 35(8):2387-2399.

O'Day, S. J., P. O'Day, and D. W. Steadman. 2003. "Defining the Lau
    Context: Recent Findings on Nayau, Lau Islands, Fiji." *New
    Zealand Journal of Archaeology* 25:31-56.

Pandolfi, J. M., J. B. C. Jackson, N. Baron, R. H. Bradbury, H. M.
    Guzman, T. P. Hughes, C. V. Kappel, F. Micheli, J. C. Ogden,
    H. P. Possingham, and E. Sala. 2005. "Are U.S. Coral Reefs
    on the Slippery Slope to Slime?" *Science* 307:1725-1726.

Pawley, A., and R. Green. 1973. "Dating the Dispersal of the Oceanic
    Languages." *Oceanic Linguistics* 12(1):1-67.

Pietrusewsky, Michael, Michele T. Douglas, Ethan E. Cochrane, and
    Scott Reinke. 2007. "Cultural Modifications in an
    Adolescent Earth-oven Interment from Fiji: Sorting out
    Mortuary Practice." *Journal of Island and Coastal
    Archaeology* 2(1):44-71.

Rathje, William J. and Cullen Murphy. 2001. *Rubbish! The
    Archaeology of Garbage.* Tucson: University of Arizona
    Press.

Schiffer, Michael B. 1972. "Archaeological Context and Systemic
    Context." *American Antiquity* 37(2):156-165.

Schwartz, Theodore. 1976. "The Cargo Cult: A Melanesian
    Type-Response to Change." In *Responses to Change*, edited
    by George A. DeVos, 157-206. New York: D. Van Nostrand.

Shaw, I., and R. Jameson. 1999. *A Dictionary of Archaeology*. Oxford: Blackwell.

Steadman, David W., Susan C. Anton, and Patrick V. Kirch. 2000. "Ana Manuku: A Prehistoric Ritualistic Site On Mangaia, Cook Islands." *Antiquity* 74:873-83.

Thomas, Nicholas. 1991. *Entangled Objects: Exchange, Material Culture, and Colonialism in the Pacific*. Cambridge: Harvard University Press.

Toren, Christina. 1988. "Making the Present, Revealing the Past: The Mutability and Continuity of Tradition as Process." *Man*, New Series 23(4):696-717.

————. 2007. "Sunday Lunch in Fiji: Continuity and Transformation in Ideas of the Household." *American Anthropologist* 109(2):285-95.

USDE (United States Department of Education). 2006. "A Test of Leadership: Charting the Future of U.S. Higher Education." http://www.ed.gov/about/bdscomm/list/ hiedfuture/ reports/final-report.pdf.

Worsley, Peter. 1957. *The Trumpet Shall Sound: A Study of 'Cargo' Cults in Melanesia*. London: MacGibbon and Kee.

Making Africa Accessible: Bringing Guinea-Bissau into the University Classroom

Brandon D. Lundy

OVERVIEW

A growing literature documents Africa's history, its cultural diversity, and its contemporary trends. Meanwhile, accessible work on educational initiatives by individuals and institutions tackling problems of Afro-pessimism and Afro-ignorance are less common and yet no less important. This chapter gives examples of how firsthand ethnographic research in Africa can be brought into the classroom to foster a better understanding across the US/Africa cultural divide. What follows connects ground-level practices in a marginalized part of the world with issues that matter to American university students. Topics under discussion include: (1) female circumcision, (2) what makes a successful plural society, (3) religious syncretism, and (4) local links to global history. These themes are described in relation to a small village in southern Guinea-Bissau. This chapter demonstrates how American students can come to understand how Africa's civil society is successfully navigating the margins of globalizing terrains.

INTRODUCTION

My brother came to visit me during my yearlong fieldwork in Guinea-Bissau, West Africa, in 2007. It was his first trip outside of the United States. He was making this journey in part to better inform his pedagogy as a middle school social studies teacher. Each year, he was required to dedicate one month to teaching the African continent. His lesson plans, pulled from a few textbook chapters, were often his students' first and only formal exposure to Africa over the next two years. As a university-level anthropology professor, I am acutely aware of the prodigious underexposure to "Africa" throughout the American education system, often further compounding misconceptions and stereotypes about the continent. I, therefore, wanted my brother's experience to reflect the people I had come to know and respect, not the Western conceptions of exoticism and pessimism portrayed in the media, popular culture, and, regrettably, middle school textbooks.

In a similar vein, this chapter explores some of my own pedagogical practices in an attempt to make "Africa" accessible to an American audience. I do this by focusing on how I nurture specific partnerships between my research fieldsite community in southwestern Guinea-Bissau and my classrooms back in Kennesaw, Georgia. Before proceeding further, let me provide some necessary background about Guinea-Bissau and my home institution of Kennesaw State University.

About Guinea-Bissau

Guinea-Bissau is located along the Upper Guinea Coast of West Africa and shares a border with Senegal to the north and Guinea Conakry to the east. With a population of just over 1.5 million, Guinea-Bissau is a patchwork of approximately 33 different ethnic groups (Davidson 2002, 419).

Africanist historian Walter Rodney describes the people of Guinea-Bissau as refugees driven from their positions in the hinterland, who eventually settled along the coast where the mangroves and thick forests offered some natural protections from invaders (1970, 8).

Today's plural society is a consequence of the Mali Empire's expansion during the eleventh century, the subsequent rise of the semiautonomous kingdom of Kaabu, as well as European contact, Portuguese colonialism, and a protracted struggle for independence. Contemporary ethnic groups of Guinea-Bissau are "marked by a particular identity, history, language, cultural traits, and other distinct social features" (Forrest 2003, 28). Simultaneously, the overlapping history and cultural traditions, such as the shared Kriol language and nationalist sentiments, suggest complex webs of "multiethnic alliances, social linkages, and political ties" (Forrest 2003, 28), continuously fashioned, sustained, and abandoned throughout the centuries. As the country's most influential revolutionary leader, Amílcar Cabral (1924-1973) helped to eliminate the Portuguese colonial presence in both Cape Verde and Guinea-Bissau through armed struggle, while his intellectual efforts helped to create and unite a pluralistic society and undermine imperialism internationally (Chilcote 1991, 3). Cabral helped to cultivate national unity within Guinea-Bissau's context of diversity.

The medley of ethnic groups making up Guinea-Bissau suggests to many contemporary scholars a potential site for research on heterogeneity, interethnic conflict, national destabilization, and balkanization. Anthropologist Joanna Davidson (2002, 419), however, remarks on the uncanny and "perplexing realization" that what one actually finds in the scholarly literature is that "relatively little interethnic conflict exists," and, she continues, "attention to ... ethnic based rivalries ... is far outweighed by the recurring trope of Guinea-Bissau as a successful plural society." I revisit this seeming contradiction later in the chapter.

It is within this context that I illustrate my research site (pop. 676), located in the Cacine sector of Guinea-Bissau's southernmost Tombali region, for my American students. This area is considered to be the patrimony of the recently Islamicized Nalú ethnic group, who claim territorial hegemony as the area's first settlers. The Nalú population is divided by state borders between Guinea-Bissau and Guinea Conakry. They number less than 25,000 worldwide, with 134 living in two distinct neighborhoods in the research community. The other four neighborhoods support 542 spiritist Balanta who began to immigrate into the Cacine sector in 1939 from the northern Nhacra sector in search of food and arable land.

The Balanta are the single largest ethnic group in Guinea-Bissau, making up more than 30 percent of the entire population. They are generally considered egalitarian in sociopolitical organization (Hawthorne 2003). The Balanta continue to practice their own traditional religion, keep livestock, and cultivate rice. Although they find themselves in almost all corners of the country, Marina Padrão Temudo believes that the Balanta maintain an "isolationist rationale" (2009, 49) because they do not participate in trade networks, they value agricultural production over education, and they privilege their ethnic language over the more widely spoken Portuguese Kriol and ethnic Susu. Initiation is tightly controlled by the Balanta elders. At the same time, Balanta make up the majority of Guinea-Bissau's military and are involved to some degree in local and national politics.

About Kennesaw State University

Originally founded in 1963 as Kennesaw Junior College, by 2009 Kennesaw State University (KSU) was the third-largest university in Georgia, with students representing more than 140 countries (www.kennesaw.edu). The university's main campus is located in Kennesaw, Georgia, approximately 20 miles northwest of Atlanta.

KSU's commitment to expanding the global experience of students, faculty, and staff is demonstrated by the 2007

Quality Enhancement Plan (QEP) known as the "Get Global" initiative, focused on increasing opportunities for international learning experiences. By the spring of 2009, KSU awarded its first Global Engagement Certification to qualified students in recognition of their achievements in learning global perspectives and intercultural skills development.

KSU is a diverse mixture of traditional and nontraditional, residential and commuter students. For example, 31 percent of the students enrolled in 2010 identified as something other than "White, Non-Hispanic Origin," while 6 percent were foreign nationals. Of these, 379 students self-reported their countries of origin to be one of 33 different African countries, with the top five being Nigeria (110 students), Kenya (86 students), Ghana (35 students), Cameroon (28 students), and South Africa (25 students) (KSU Fact Book 2010).

As of fall 2009, KSU employed 701 full-time and 553 part-time faculty. KSU's Africanist faculty are found in more than 12 different departments and programs across several colleges, with expertise in more than 25 different African nations. The university supports an African and African Diaspora Studies program (AADS), in which many of these Africanists are affiliated. This depth of diversity and understanding about the African continent at KSU provides the faculty and students with an ideal site to continue to think about the relationships between the United States and Africa.

Pedagogical Approach

It is within this diverse institutional setting that I begin each of my courses by suggesting to the students that after sitting through my class, they should take away an appreciation for both humanity's differences and similarities. My teaching, supervision, and mentoring are measured and evaluated according to two simple axioms that inform my scholarship: (1) a unity exists between theory and practice and (2) educational experiences are processual in nature. I build on these axioms by encouraging contact between myself and students, developing reciprocity and cooperation among students, and encouraging active learning. I respect diverse talents, worldviews, and ways of learning among the student body by encouraging respectful classroom discussions among students after providing them with appropriate exposure to both competing and complementary materials on a given topic.

Similar to what is often experienced when doing ethnographic research, teachers face a wide range of attitudes, requiring sensitivity, patience, and tact. Teaching is more than the transference of knowledge and skills. Teaching involves nurturing critical thinking and giving students the resources to educate themselves in a safe environment. I believe that effective teaching must be primarily planned and conducted from the learner's point of view.

It is with these pedagogical sentiments that I attempted to expand my brother's own worldview and teaching repertoire by trying to arrange a successful interaction between my co-workers in Guinea-Bissau and my brother.

Once my brother landed in the capital city of Bissau, we made our way to the neighborhood of *Bairro Militar* where we would be spending the night at a friend's house. I brought my brother a bucket of water to freshen up after his long journey. It was to be his first outdoor bucket bath. He stepped behind the three cement walls and rusted metal door. Shortly thereafter, to his dismay, 20 neighborhood kids congregated outside and began to make quite a commotion. When my brother, with his American modesty, finally exited the outdoor shower area, he was further unnerved when he saw a dead "bush rat" that had been flushed from the drain. He quickly realized that the neighbor kids were killing the rat for its meat, not peeping through the crack in the door. (See Photograph 6.1.)

Photograph 6.1. Bush rat meal. Photograph by Brandon Lundy.

To my chagrin, with this incident I feared that many of those African stereotypes deeply embedded in my brother's psyche were being reinforced, not dispelled. Similar difficulties arise when I am attempting to nurture critical thinking about the peoples and cultures of Africa in my own university classrooms. Challenging our preconceptions is a slow process, but the reward for thinking in cross-cultural terms about our ethnocentricities as well as our commonalities with other peoples is a valuable and necessary undertaking. So how can American educators go about changing these systematic stereotypes about the more than 50 countries and territories of Africa on both the individual and institutional levels? Further, what is the pedagogical value in such an undertaking?

TEACHING AFRICA IN THE TWENTY-FIRST CENTURY
CLASSROOM

Beginning in the 1960s, works about studying and, to a lesser degree, teaching Africa in the United States have been sponsored rou-
tinely by the African Studies Association (ASA), inspired primarily
from a desire to better understand the newly emerging independent
African nations. The focus of much of this early scholarship revolved
around issues of cultural studies and the viability of African Studies
programs in the United States after World War II (Alpers & Roberts
2002; Bowman 2002; Bowman and Cohen 2002; Guyer et al. 1996;
McCann 2002; Vengroff 2002; Zeleza 1997).

By 2002, real revisions to traditional African studies in the
United States were underway. For example, James C. McCann built
upon Jane I. Guyer's 1996 history of the African Studies movement in
order to account for the most recent trends in which African studies
moved beyond the federally funded area studies programs (i.e., Title
VI) toward a "polycentric academic landscape" (2002, 35-36). This
polycentric landscape of African pedagogy promotes the teaching of
African issues to a wider US student-base with a greater potential
for challenging misconceptions and stereotypes about the peoples
and cultures of Africa. These histories were backed by several brief
opinion pieces in the literature about teaching Africa to US undergraduates at a number of academic institutions and settings (Alpers
1995; Ansell 2002; Robson 2002; Thornton 2000).

Besides general works on African studies, it is not uncommon
to find contributions in the literature dealing specifically with Africa in relation to particular disciplinary paradigms. One example
of how the social sciences focus on Africa is Robert H. Bates et al.'s
edited volume *Africa and the Disciplines: The Contributions of Research in Africa to the Social Sciences and Humanities* (1993), which

contains Sally Falk Moore's famous essay "Changing Perspectives on a Changing Africa: The Work of Anthropology" (3-57). Sally Falk Moore extends this argument in her book-length piece *Anthropology and Africa: Changing Perspectives on a Changing Scene*, which is "intended for people who are interested in Africa, in anthropology, in the history of ideas, or in all three" (1994, vii).

Advancing the field of study between Africa and anthropology even further, Mwenda Ntaragwi, David Mills, and Mustafa Babiker's edited volume *African Anthropologies: History, Critique and Practice* (2006) attempts to bridge the gap between Africa and the United States through an indigenous perspective on anthropology in Africa. It focuses on the history of anthropological training on the continent. These and similar works, however, remain limited in scope and often do not reach audiences outside of their own fields of study.

The literature on the scholarship of teaching and learning, on the other hand, has the potential to impact a much larger audience. The two most comprehensive multi- or cross-disciplinary works to date on the topic of teaching Africa to US undergraduates are Curtis Keim's *Mistaking Africa: Curiosities and Inventions of the American Mind* (2009) and Misty L. Bastian and Jane L. Parpart's edited volume *Great Ideas for Teaching about Africa* (1999). These resources are important for several reasons. First, they are multi- and cross-disciplinary, which makes them relevant to a larger number of individuals as well as broader in scope. Second, these books help to dispel mistaken assumptions and provide solid illustrations for teaching about Africa in a more appropriate and nuanced way.

Keim's book, for example, is primarily dedicated to discussing what Africa is not. He suggests that "even if we want to avoid portraying Africa in stereotypical terms, we are bound to do so because we have few other models of Africa to which we can compare these images" (2009, 32). Keim argues that for a majority of Americans,

Africa and its people are simply marginal and often left out of the discussion altogether. This greatly worries him: "If, for example, we are wrong about Africa's supposed insignificance, we will be blindsided by political, environmental, or even medical events that affect how we survive" (2009, 4). This hints at why Americans should care about issues beyond our egocentric interests, as demonstrated through the *tragedy of the commons*, where the immediate gratification of a few is mitigated through the dispersal of consequences over an entire population. As educators, we must consider global implications of our thoughts and actions (in both time and space) and then convey both the results of this exercise as well as the critical exercise itself to our students. In the case of Africa, Keim (2009, 9) continues, "We also perpetuate negative myths about Africa because they help us maintain dominance over Africans.... It doesn't take much imagination to figure out that modern Americans who deal with Africa—bureaucrats, aid workers, businesspeople, missionaries, and others—might have an interest in describing Africa in ways that justify the importance of their own."

Keim sheds light on these myths; for him, Africa becomes a cognitive exercise used to dispel misconceptions held by students. Keim's book is primarily dedicated to refuting the many stereotypes Americans hold about Africa. He concludes by advocating for a renewed focus on diversity and respectful dialogue when it comes to Africa-centered pedagogy without saying how to achieve this important goal.

The second volume mentioned above, Bastian and Parpart's (1999, 1) edited volume on teaching about Africa, is a wonderful pedagogical resource. Their volume demonstrates how "university-level instructors bring African issues and topics into their classrooms, breaking down stereotypical notions about the continent and engaging students with the variety, scope, and potential of societies on one of the largest continents of the world." While the book is an excellent next step in teaching following from Keim's work, unfortunately, it is now more than 10 years old, and an update on Africa's most recent global influence is now necessary. Much has changed in Western–African relations in the last 10 years including the rethinking of the neoliberal policies of the 1990s, the further advance of globalization, the rise of China, the development of AFRICOM, and much, much more. There have also been a number of new crises that students may have heard about; for example, the situations in Darfur and Congo, that merit classroom attention.

Why We Need Africa

Africa, the world's second-largest and second-most-populous continent, surpassing one billion people today, is globally important, whether recognized as such by Americans or not. Africa is the birthplace of the human species, saw the rise and fall of some of the most powerful and far-reaching empires the world has ever known, and today has some of the Earth's richest natural resources. Divided into 54 nations and territories, the African continent covers approximately 20 percent of the Earth's total surface area. It is estimated that over 1,000 languages can be heard there. By 2050, one in every five people worldwide will be African.

The histories of the United States and Africa have been interwoven for more than five centuries. Today, the United States is cautiously forging new partnerships on the continent. Meanwhile, since the mid-1990s, China has made an all-out effort to gain favor in Africa, with considerable success. China's influence is even surpassing that of the United States in some countries (Hilsum 2005; Klare and Volman 2006; Sautman and Hairong 2007; Seddon 2006; Taylor 1998; Tull 2006). Clearly, the continent of Africa is a major international player, with its future having global stakes. And yet, for many American students, Africa remains the *Dark Continent*. So how can African specialists turn the spotlight on this fascinating and varied continent?

Collaboration among Africanists, students, and more than one billion Africans is our strongest option to encourage critical thinking about the continent. How can college and university students learn to recognize and incorporate the similarities, differences, and interconnections between the peoples of Africa and the United States? How can teacher-scholars foster global citizens who demonstrate respect and support for the common good of a diverse world community? And why bring African issues into Western, specifically US, classrooms? Let me briefly discuss three perspectives that I think are key.

First, students must begin to disaggregate Africa into its highly variable, and sometimes volatile, nations, states, cultural groups, institutions, and the like. In this way, they will begin to understand continental particularities that may or may not affect the entire global system and vice versa. This includes matters such as anti-Islamic sentiments here in the United States, issues of US military and strategic concern (Besteman 2008; Keenan 2008), petroleum needs (Klare and Volman 2006), and the war on drugs (Ellis 2009; International Crisis Group 2009; Singer 2008; UNODC 2007, 2008), just to name a few.

Second, on the individual level, an active research agenda is a strong enhancer of teaching effectiveness. Being able to speak about a research agenda from start to finish, with the kind of expertise that only comes from one's own projects, is a wonderful, scholarly way to get students interested in a subject. It also lets them see the relevance of the work they are doing in class. While it is certainly possible to teach about culture and methodology without bringing up one's own research, I find that the topics come alive in class when lectures and in-class activities are based on personal experience. This often motivates students to read more and to consider further involvement in Africa and African issues. These classroom engagements help students understand what is occurring at the ground level in specific contexts, something they often cannot discover on their own, due to inadequate or out-dated library materials.

Third, teaching about Africa is a critical and a personal undertaking for those 35 million African Americans and more than 2.2 million foreign-born blacks in the United States today (Morris 2003, 255-256). For them, US and world history often fails to capture their multiple and overlapping political and historical experiences as people of African ancestry.

Africa is no longer simply a journalistic prop in the United States used to convey tales of the primitive "other." I tend to agree with Nicola Ansell (2002, 357) when she writes, "What is needed, therefore, is a way of helping students interrogate their own images of Africa: to explore their origins, the ways they reflect historical and contemporary power relations and their relationships to the material circumstances of African people's lives."

Today, Africa is a continent on the rise in industry, technology, population, and innovation. Africa also has a rich and diverse history, which must be deeply explored and understood by any global institution looking to cultivate African understanding and alliances. Keim (2009, 12) reminds us, "Africa, because of its sheer size, population, resources, and modernization, will play an increasingly important role in the world, whether for good or ill, and will have to be taken seriously. Our long-term interest in our shrinking world is to understand Africa with as little bias as possible." Just as importantly, Africa is diverse and offers alternatives to Western philosophy in political, economic, religious, and social thinking.

When it comes to teaching, I utilize my field research and advocacy to demonstrate to my students how diverse cultures can inform our own understanding of ourselves. Teaching is more than the transference of knowledge and skills. Teaching involves nurturing alternative worldviews and giving students the resources to educate themselves in a safe environment. The following are four classroom activities that I use to make Africa both accessible and relevant to my students by bringing Guinea-Bissau into the university classroom:

CLASSROOM APPROACHES

Female Circumcision

In order to expose a broader swath of students to African issues, the first exercise that I will discuss actually takes place in an undergraduate course not specifically related to the continent, called "Social Issues in Cultural Anthropology." As the name implies, the course critically examines a common set of world social issues from an anthropological perspective. I begin with the hot button issue of female circumcision early in the semester to engage the students and to get them thinking in new ways. Although not a uniquely African phenomenon, many students incorrectly associate the practice with the continent, primarily as a result of high-profile media attention to African cases (e.g., Waris Dirie of Somalia) and general misinformation. As the particulars of the issues are examined, I foster a broader discussion of the topic in order to provide specific context for a debate over universal human rights versus cultural relativism. I also use this topic as a way to discuss the themes of power, agency, oppression, and resistance.

General discussion about female circumcision would be less useful without specific examples. Therefore, I provide students an example of a particular case. First, after an appropriate warning to the class about the graphic nature of what I am about to present, I read a chapter titled "Cutting Time" from Mende Nazer's 2003 autobiography *Slave: My True Story*. In this chapter, Nazer, a member of the Nuba people of the Sudan, recounts her infibulation in graphic detail. By the conclusion of the story, I find that most students who previously had relativistic tendencies, or no opinion, have now begun to question their views.

I then start to muddy their convictions by discussing a short piece from the December 28, 1996, *New York Times* titled "Tug of Taboos: African Genital Rite vs. American Law," written by Celia W. Dugger. This article investigates the precarious bind for Somali refugees in the United States who want their daughters to be circumcised as their custom dictates even though they are forbidden to do so by US law. I ask the class why the US government has made female circumcision illegal while male circumcision is so accepted and commonplace. We also start to discuss elective and plastic surgery, such as labiaplasty or vaginoplasty, gender reassignment surgery, and the genital modification of intersexuals. We go on to talk about similarities with other forms of body modification in general, such as tattooing and piercing.

Finally, I bring the conversation to female circumcision practices in Guinea-Bissau by having them read Michelle C. Johnson's article "Making Mandinga or Making Muslim? Debating Female Circumcision, Ethnicity, and Islam in Guinea-Bissau and Portugal." The class mines the article for evidence on either side of the debate. Johnson's article starts with a conversation with Binta who states, "People say that circumcision is a bad thing for women, but we know the truth. If a woman isn't circumcised, she is unclean and her prayers are worthless. When you are circumcised, you become a true Muslim" (2007,

202). This article succeeds in adding religion and power relations into the conversation.

I conclude with an anecdote from my own ethnographic experience among the Nalú of southern Guinea-Bissau. When I first broached the topic of female circumcision with my closest Nalú friend and colleague in 2007, she said that they used to practice cutting in the past until Americans arrived in the village in the 1990s and "educated" them about the health risks and patriarchal implications of such customs. I was told that since that time, they had discontinued the practice.

Several months later after a hard day of working in the paddy rice fields; however, I learned from two fathers in the village that their youngest daughters had just gone through their *finadu* (a week-long rite of passage into female adulthood, including circumcision) the previous year, even though it was against the fathers' wishes. I was eventually told by both male and female elders that the practice was a fairly recent thing among the Nalú, only found since their conversion to Islam in the twentieth century. It was currently being practiced by the female elders as a means of maintaining spiritual equality between the genders, a central part of traditional religion as demonstrated in their secret societies and the configuration of their sacred groves. The continued practice was later corroborated when I witnessed a group of young girls from a neighboring village go through the rite. (See Photograph 6.2.)

Photograph 6.2. Female Initiation Rites. Photograph by Brandon Lundy.

Finally, female circumcision in Guinea-Bissau was not always as ideologically motivated as many Americans would believe. In fact, I documented instances of girls from non-Islamic ethnic groups that did not practice circumcision who voluntarily accompanied their Muslim friends through the rite without parental consent. This suggests forms of inter-group peer pressure as a motivating factor in a girl's decision to become circumcised. This anecdote introduces another facet to the conversation, one of gender roles. It contradicts the long-held argument that female circumcision was a practice invented by men to control women's sexuality and wombs in order to guarantee the legitimacy of their offspring.

Guinea-Bissau as a Successful Plural Society?

I introduce another topic related to Africa in my undergraduate class "Cultures and Societies of the World." I begin with a classroom discussion by asking the following questions: (1) Does interethnic contact inevitably lead to assimilation or conflict? Why or why not? And (2) Are successful plural societies (i.e., societies combining ethnic contrasts, ecological specialization, and the economic interdependence of groups) possible? What makes you think this way?

Next, I provide my students with a slide show and lecture about my own research among Guinea-Bissau's Nalú and Balanta. The students are then asked to write a one-page essay based on their predictions about what they see happening to Guinea-Bissau and my research community over the next 10 years. To facilitate this exercise, I provide the students with background information like that given earlier in the chapter about the country's ethnic makeup and unique history.

Although the Nalú and Balanta differ substantially, they have been living in close proximity in southern Guinea-Bissau for almost a century. The Balanta would often tell me that the Nalú are a diffident people whose villages remain close-knit, and semi-isolated. A majority of Nalú marriages are endogamous, and the Nalú retain a profound knowledge of the forest as powerful healers and herbalists. I was told that the Nalú don't think like the rest of the world; "They are contrary." "The Nalú are like a snake entering its hole. You think it goes in head first and you can grab it. But, it actually back tracks with its head to protect itself. No matter how close you get, you will never really know the Nalú's true nature" (personal communication, 09/01/2007). At the same time, the Nalú describe their Balanta neighbors as thieves and drunks, both in reference to their cultural traditions involving alcohol as non-Muslims and to attempts by Balanta youths to demonstrate their prowess and readiness for their own initiation into adulthood by stealing cattle. And yet, the Balanta and Nalú of the research community seem to successfully coexist.

Because it is sometimes difficult for Western students to understand why cooperation may be a better strategy than competition in some cases, I conclude the class with a game that demonstrates lessons from game theory. This "X/Y" game is a modified version of *The Prisoner's Dilemma* in which small groups explore the results of embracing collaboration in opposition to competition. Western culture has reinforced the idea that "winning" is all about the individual or team and dominating other individuals or teams. In this activity, if the cooperative path is chosen, all involved will experience the optimal outcome. Due to our competitive nature, however, what ensues instead, in the classroom is an arms race where, eventually, all involved lose. This activity encourages critical thinking, interpersonal and conceptual skills, communication skills, and global perspectives and engagement.

Religious Syncretism

Like most anthropologists, I discuss belief systems and religion in my "Introduction to Cultural Anthropology" course. By way of introducing the topic, I like to show a section of the documentary *Zeitgeist* that focuses on the syncretic origins of Christianity. My hope is that students will then start to think about religious systems as blended, or syncretic, instead of as discreet cosmologies that were independently invented. I then move into a discussion of differences between monotheistic and polytheistic religions. Specifically, I draw my students' attention to the fact that monotheistic religions are inherently inflexible because according to their doctrine there can only be "one true God." Polytheistic religions, on the other hand, are inherently flexible and accepting of others' deities since they are often specialized, personal, and accessible. I then start a class-wide discussion by asking the students to consider what may result when a monotheistic religious system comes into contact with a polytheistic one, such as what occurred when European missionaries began to visit Africa starting in the fifteenth century.

Next, I provide my students with an illustration of religious syncretism by discussing my research in Guinea-Bissau, a country whose religious make-up is described as approximately 45 percent indigenous beliefs, 50 percent Muslim, and 5 percent Christian, although a high degree of blending among these three belief systems is closer to reality.

I mention to the class that during my own ethnographic fieldwork, I documented the Islamic Nalú maintaining contacts with their ancestors at the *baloba* or sacred grove. I do this through both a brief lecture about the history of conversion in my research area and by talking about my own experiences through a slide show from my personal collection of images. (See Photograph 6.3.)

Photograph 6.3. The author learning about the sacred grove. Photograph by Brandon Lundy.

During this lecture, I ask students to think about their own beliefs. We conclude the lesson by discussing how, even within our own seemingly inflexible monotheistic religious systems, there is room to negotiate our beliefs. I also draw their attention to the complex, yet significant, interrelationships between social structure, religion, economics, and politics.

Local Links to Global History

Another strategy that I employ in the classroom, and the last one that I will discuss in this chapter, is to draw parallels between my research in West Africa, historical assumptions, and my students' localized knowledge. One way that I do this at KSU is by linking West African coastal rice production to Georgia's agricultural history. For example, I introduce my students to the ethnographic fieldwork and historical linguistics of Edda Fields-Black (2008). She traces the prehistoric origins and development of tidal rice production along West Africa's Rice Coast, particularly in the Rio Nunez region of coastal Guinea and explores its transfer to the New World during the transAtlantic slave trade, particularly to South Carolina and Georgia. (See Photograph 6.4.)

Photograph 6.4. Rice planting. Photograph by Brandon Lundy.

Fields-Black builds on Judith A. Carney's 2001 groundbreaking work *Black Rice: The African Origins of Rice Cultivation in the Americas.* Carney demonstrates through an exhaustive exploration into the historical and botanical records that the African rice knowledge system diffused across the Atlantic, shaping the cultures of the Americas beginning as early as the sixteenth century.

In encountering Carney's many discoveries, students are often most surprised to learn that Thomas Jefferson experimented with red *Orzya glabberima* rice from the uplands of Guinea in West Africa in his search for a successful alternative to the lowland variety under cultivation in Virginia. He wished to move away from the lowland tidal swamps where the deadly effects of malaria, also imported from West Africa during the Transatlantic Slave Trade, were being felt. I recommend that my students visit the exhibit at the Black Madonna cultural center in downtown Atlanta that displays a flyer of a slave auction held in Georgia that advertised "slaves with rice knowledge" for sale.

We go on to discuss various ethnic groups' roles in the Transatlantic Slave Trade and how these same Africans played a part in shaping contemporary Georgia by making historical and localized connections. Confronting students with revised histories (Thornton 2000) provides them with valuable lessons and a critical tool kit on which to draw inspiration when questioning Eurocentric accounts of world history throughout their academic careers.

CONCLUSION: ONE WEEK LATER ...

Changing people's attitudes about anything is not an easy task. Changing long-held stereotypes that have pervaded popular culture proves especially difficult. Many Africanists are taking on this very task because they realize the implications of not recognizing the global significance of such a large and diverse continent as Africa. Educators at all levels are beginning to innovate the teaching of cultural studies, especially in relation to so many potential cross-cultural partnerships. Let me conclude by returning to my brother's visit to Guinea-Bissau in his attempt to bring real insights on Africa into his middle school social studies class.

After an exceptional evening meal that consisted of goat served five different ways, my brother and I turned in for the night. We were given the only room in the cement house with a door, which turned out to be the master suite. Hospitality is a way of life in Guinea-Bissau, and my brother was overwhelmed by our hosts' generosity. That night we slept comfortably under our mosquito net, with an electric fan keeping us cool. We awoke to bucket baths and a breakfast of goat while we waited for the car that would take us southward. After an exhausting drive lasting all day, we finally arrived at my field site that evening.

As had been my original experience, the villagers warmly welcomed my brother. He had the opportunity to visit the local schoolhouse, play football with the neighborhood kids, swim at the nearby beach, and attempt to communicate in broken Spanish with the villagers' Portuguese-based Kriol. They held a dance in his honor; and, being a fraternity brother, he drank cashew wine with the neighboring spiritist Balanta villagers. He spent the remainder of his days in Guinea-Bissau finding the "familiar in the strange" as we moved about the country until it was time for him to return home.

It is this lesson that he now conveys to his students in his middle school classroom. He no longer solely teaches Africa from the textbook. My brother teaches his students about the village in southern Guinea-Bissau where he attended school, played football, danced, swam, and even drank the local wine. He portrays the story of his visit through a slide show and helps his students begin to recognize the "familiar in the strange," as he had done. "We are all humans with certain needs," he says. "It is just how we go about meeting those needs that can change from place to place."

This is just one of the many reasons there needs to be a change in the US education system at all levels in an attempt to "pluralize the curriculum" (Hilliard III 1991) by teaching Africa in the classroom. This chapter builds on the work of more traditional African Studies programs by promoting the teaching of African themes in a wider array of courses, not just those dedicated to Africa. As the need to understand the diverse patterns and processes of African peoples increases in the United States in order for our students to become better global citizens who are able to engage with a global world system, this polycentric attitude toward teaching at the university level is currently our strongest approach. By collaborating across the disciplines, and across the Atlantic, a new multi-positioned discourse allows teachers and students to draw on different perspectives that bear upon the study of Africa, leading to a developed capacity to think critically about the world around us.

REFERENCES

Alpers, Edward A. 1995. "Reflections on the Studying and Teaching about Africa in America." *Issue: A Journal of Opinion* 23(1): 9-10.

———, and Allen F. Roberts. 2002. "What is African Studies? Some Reflections." *African Issues* 30(2):11-18.

Ansell, Nicola. 2002. "Using Films in Teaching About Africa." *Journal of Geography in Higher Education* 26(3):355-368.

Bastian, Misty L., and Jane L. Parpart, eds. 1999. *Great Ideas for Teaching about Africa.* Boulder, CO: Lynne Rienner.

Besteman, Catherine. 2008. "'Beware of Those Bearing Gifts': An Anthropologist's View of Africom." *Anthropology Today* 24(5):20-21.

Bowman, Larry W., ed. 2002. "Identifying New Directions for African Studies." *African Issues* 30(2).

———, and Diana T. Cohen. 2002. "Identifying New Directions for African Studies: The National Survey of African Studies." *African Issues* 30(2):2-10.

Carney, Judith A. 2001. *Black Rice: The African Origins of Rice Cultivation in the Americas*. Cambridge, MA: Harvard University Press.

Chilcote, Ronald H. 1991. *Amílcar Cabral's Revolutionary Theory and Practice: A Critical Guide*. Boulder, CO: Lynne Rienner.

Davidson, Joanna. 2002. "Plural Society and Interethnic Relations in Guinea-Bissau." In *Engaging Cultural Differences: The Multicultural Challenge in Liberal Democracies*, edited by R. A. Shweder, M. Minow, and H. R. Markus, 417-431. New York: Russell Sage Foundation.

Dugger, Celia W. 1996. "Tug of Taboos: African Genital Rite vs. American Law." *New York Times*, December 28.

Ellis, Stephen. 2009. "West Africa's International Drug Trade." *African Affairs* 108(431):171-196.

Fields-Black, Edda L. 2008. *Deep Roots: Rice Farmers in West Africa and the African Diaspora*. Bloomington: Indiana University Press.

Forrest, Joshua B. 2003. *Lineages of State Fragility: Rural Civil Society in Guinea-Bissau*. Athens: Ohio University Press.

Freire, Paulo. 1978. *Pedagogy in Process: The Letters to Guinea-Bissau*, translated by C. St. John Hunter. New York: Seabury Press.

Guyer, Jane I., with Akbar M. Virmani, and Amanda Kemp. 1996. *African Studies in the United States: A Perspective*. Atlanta: African Studies Association Press.

Hawthorne, Walter. 2003. *Planting Rice and Harvesting Slaves: Transformations along the Guinea-Bissau Coast, 1400-1900*. Portsmouth, NH: Heinemann.

Hilliard III, Asa G. 1991. "Why We Must Pluralize the Curriculum." *Educational Leadership* 49(4):12-14.

———, L. Patyon-Steward, and L. Obadele, eds. 1990. *The Infusion of African and African American Content in the School Curriculum*. Morristown, NJ: Aaron Press.

Hilsum, Lindsey. 2005. "Re-Enter the Dragon: China's New Mission in Africa." *Review of African Political Economy* 32(104/105):419-425.

International Crisis Group. 2009. "Guinea-Bissau: Building a Real Stability Pact." *Policy/Africa Briefing* 57(January 29):1-16.

Johnson, Michelle C. 2007. "Making Mandinga or Making Muslim? Debating Female Circumcision, Ethnicity, and Islam in Guinea-Bissau and Portugal." In *Transcultural Bodies: Female Genital Cutting in Global Context*, edited by Y. Hernlund and B. Shell-Duncan, 202-223. New Brunswick, NJ: Rutgers University Press.

Keenan, Jeremy. 2008. "US Militarization in Africa: What Anthropologists Should Know about AFRICOM." *Anthropology Today* 24(5):16-20.

Keim, Curtis. 2009. *Mistaking Africa: Curiosities and Inventions of the American Mind*. 2nd ed. Boulder, CO: Westview Press.

Klare, Michael, and Daniel Volman. 2006. "America, China and the Scramble for Africa's Oil." *Review of African Political Economy* 33(108):297-309.

McCann, James C. 2002. "Title VI and African Studies: Prospects in a Polycentric Academic Landscape." *African Issues* 30(2):30-36.

Moore, Sally Falk. 1993. "Changing Perspectives on a Changing Africa: The Work of Anthropology." In *Africa and the Disciplines: The Contributions of Research in Africa to the Social Sciences and Humanities*, edited by R. H. Bates, V. Y. Mudimbe, and J. O'Barr, 3-57. Chicago: University of Chicago Press.

———. 1994. *Anthropology and Africa: Changing Perspectives on a Changing Scene*. Charlottesville: University Press of Virginia.

Morris, Jerome E. 2003. "What Does Africa Have to Do with Being African American? A Microethnographic Analysis of a Middle School Inquiry Unit on Africa." *Anthropology and Education Quarterly* 34(3):255-276.

Nazer, Mende, and Damien Lewis. 2003. *Slave: My True Story*. New York: Public Affairs.

Ntarangwi, Mwenda, David Mills, and Mustafa Babiker, eds. 2006. *African Anthropologies: History, Critique and Practice*. Dakar: CODESRIA.

Robson, Elsbeth. 2002. "'An Unbelievable Academic and Personal Experience': Issues around Teaching Undergraduate Field Courses in Africa." *Journal of Geography in Higher Education* 26(3):327-344.

Rodney, Walter. 1970. *A History of the Upper Guinea Coast, 1545 to 1800*. New York: Monthly Review Press.

Sautman, Barry, and Yan Hairong. 2007. "Friends and Interests: China's Distinctive Links with Africa." *African Studies Review* 50(3):75-114.

Seddon, David. 2006. "China: Africa's New Business Partner."
    Review of African Political Economy 33(110):747-749.

Singer, Merrill. 2008. *Drugs and Development: The Global Impact
    on Sustainable Growth and Human Rights.* Long Grove, IL:
    Waveland Press.

Taylor, Ian. 1998. "China's Foreign Policy towards Africa in the
    1990s." *Journal of Modern African Studies* 36(3):443-460.

Temudo, Marina Padrão. 2008. *From 'People's Struggle' to 'This War
    of Today': Entanglements of Peace and Conflict in Guinea-
    Bissau. Africa* 78(2):245-263.

———. 2009. "From the Margins of the State to the Presidential
    Palace: The Balanta Case in Guinea-Bissau." *African Studies
    Review* 52(2): 47-67.

Thornton, John. 2000. "Teaching Africa in an Atlantic Perspective."
    Radical History Review 77:123-134.

Tull, Denis M. 2006. "China's Engagement in Africa: Scope,
    Significance and Consequences." *Journal of Modern
    African Studies* 44(3):459-479.

UNODC (United Nations Office on Drugs and Crime). 2007.
    "Cocaine Trafficking in West Africa: The Threat to Stability
    and Development." www.unodc.org/documents/data-and-
    analysis/west_africa_cocaine_report_200712_en.pdf.

———. 2008. "Guinea-Bissau: A New Hub for Cocaine Trafficking."
    Perspectives 5:4-7.

Vengroff, Richard. 2002. "Retirement, Replacement, and the Future
    of African Studies." *African Issues* 30(2):57-62.

Zeleza, Paul Tiyambe. 1997. "The Perpetual Solitudes and Crises
    of African Studies in the United States." *Africa Today*
    44(2):193-210.

Causes Mini-Film Festival: Anthropology for Public Consumption

Matthew Richard and Andrea Zvikas

Every year in my Socio-Cultural Change class, I (Matthew Richard) include a requirement for an applied component, usually in the form of a group project that gives students an opportunity to apply what they are learning in class to the world outside the classroom. While I try to include such "hands on" exercises in all of my classes, I feel it is especially important to do so in a course with the word *change* in its title. In my opinion, an alluring title like "Socio-Cultural Change"—implying as it does either a gain of insight into the process of historical change, or the capability of bringing about a desired change, or better yet, a combination of both intellectual understanding and practical application—demands that we deliver on this extravagant promise. In addition to imparting the fundamentals of our subjects, we professors occasionally need to reward our budding social scientists for putting their faith in us and for committing to our academic disciplines. There's no better way to do this, I feel, than with a successful application of the subject matter. For me, this means giving students of Socio-Cultural Change the opportunity to apply their developing understanding of social forces in order to bring about transformation in our society. It's that simple.

Over the years, my students and I have made some bold attempts at making a difference, including the following ones: We made a documentary film on police brutality in our town (Richard 2002).

We surveyed the local NGO community and wrote grants on behalf of those we most admired. We did a survey of the visual content of our local newspaper over a 50-year span to determine whether race/class/gender biases were regularly depicted in the paper. And we examined how globalization was impacting our very vibrant community. These various projects always culminate in a public forum at which we share our findings with members of the community. Engaging the public and putting our knowledge to the test are nerve-racking, but gratifying, experiences for my students and me. In sharing our findings—and sometimes debating them—we feel that we are contributing to our community, and in this way, both our scientific curiosity and our humanistic urges are satisfied. I believe this double satisfaction is the reason that many social scientists are drawn to the field. The use of anthropological analysis to connect with the masses in the hope of addressing and alleviating persistent social problems is the hallmark of what has come to be called *public anthropology* (Borofsky 2007). This was the response to the widespread perception of anthropology as being among the most esoteric fields. From the 1960s to the 1990s, critics within anthropology itself charged that we wrote almost exclusively for ourselves, that we wrote books that engaged very few readers (just a few thousand students, in most instances), and that we were unconcerned with communicating with others outside the discipline. In response, public anthropology was conceived in the 1990s with the goal of addressing important social concerns and using anthropological praxis to engage the broader public.

For the past three years, I and one of my students and co-writer of this article, Andrea Zvikas, have undertaken a new project, which we've named "Causes: Valdosta State University's Mini-Film Festival." Causes invites people from all over our community—not just students—to write and produce 90-second films on issues they deem important to the community. The goal is simple: to get all of us who live in Lowndes County, Georgia, to ponder some of our casual habits and to seek better ways of doing things here. The hope is that the collective wisdom and creativity of various community members can stoke our collective imagination—maybe even our "collective conscience"—and generate improvements in our way of life. Our somewhat quixotic reasoning is that change has to start somewhere, so why not initiate it right now, right here "in our own backyard"? The production guidelines for Causes are simple: (1) produce a 90-second film in either Windows Media or Real Player; (2) write a script about a local issue; (3) introduce the film with a five-second title page, such foreshadowing makes for more parsimonious and effective narrative; (4) make sure that the sound is fully audible; and (5) avoid using music or images that are protected by copyright; instead, take your own pictures or videos and use a Web site like freeplaymusic.com for authorized background music and sound effects.

Our reasoning for the first three guidelines is the following: First, we believe that 90 seconds is an optimal length in that it is long enough to allow a story to be told effectively, yet brief enough to hold viewers' full attention. With respect to the second guideline, we discourage topics that lack a local focus because we believe that distant topics—genocide in Darfur, for example, or mountaintop removal in West Virginia—are just too easy to ignore, whereas local issues are harder to turn away from and can be addressed almost immediately. Finally, we suggest the five-second title page because we have found that such foreshadowing makes for more parsimonious and effective narrative.

The films can cover any topic, and over the past three years we've received many interesting ones on such topics as dangerous pedestrian walkways, community gardens, on-campus racism, and budget cuts to school arts programs. As social scientists, we take particular pleasure in observing the collective impressions of our participating ad hoc sociologists who have shown Causes audiences many remarkable things in the three years that our film festival has run.

My students, Andrea, and I, somewhat facetiously, refer to these films as "mini-documentaries," but in truth, the quality of the productions varies from very rough to very polished. Participants submit everything from PowerPoint presentations set to catchy pop tunes (see, in particular, http://www.youtube.com/watch?v=nD2P9qkHLDw) to high definition, multi-camera, multi-setting productions with original musical scores (see http://www.youtube.com/watch?v=RU1lfVLfJuw). Each year we have endeavored to raise the quality of the films, and in 2009 we attracted two professionals, one from New York and the other from Maine. Both, of course, produced films about issues of concern in their locales. The strategy here was that by invoking what is known as "the demonstration effect"—that is, the effect on the behavior of individuals caused by observation of the actions of others—future contributors, both in the audience as well as those viewing our films online, will aim for high production values when they make their films. We hope to attract our first European entry next year (2011); and Africa, too, is in our sights, for although we continue to wish to emphasize local problems, the videos from elsewhere enable us to learn about the problems facing other people and, more importantly, to see how they are dealing with them. Even more exciting, however, has been the involvement of several local schools.

Since the project's inception, my assistant/co-author and I have been hoping to get students of all ages involved in Causes. We visited many of the area's elementary schools and made our pitch to the principals and other administrators, and we lobbied friends working in the two area high schools and a local agricultural college. Our message was that we believe that our project has the potential to work on two very different levels. The first is straightforward and aims to take advantage of new computer technologies, namely, YouTube and Facebook, in order to disseminate a critique of a particular community social problem that is near and dear to the producers' hearts. In short, apply the critical thinking skills supposedly taught in school to identify and fix a local problem. By doing so, we aim to raise consciousness as a first step in the change process. In the making of the film *A Chorus of Fear*, I learned that a great deal of conflict occurs in society when a controversial event lacks a comprehensive and credible narrative. In the absence of such a narrative, misinformation rules, emotions run high, and tensions remain constant. I also learned that narration itself is a skill that many people don't do well; indeed, it is one that many people lack altogether. This shortcoming is particularly problematic in a town that is served by a decidedly conservative newspaper. *A Chorus of Fear* provided a credible narrative of a truly momentous local event, and people on both sides of the issue were able to understand the feelings of at least some of those on the opposing side. Through that experience, I learned that narrative succeeds because it engages the listener and causes him or her to suspend judgment, if only temporarily. That pause is precisely what is needed for any cognitive reframing to occur and, subsequently, for inter-subjectivity, which is essential to empathy, to become possible. Empathy promotes understanding and fosters respect. We believe that the Causes Mini-Film Festival can work in the same manner.

We know that Facebook has over 400 million worldwide users and that the average Facebook user has 130 friends, so that when someone reposts one of our videos—all of which are uploaded to YouTube—the message spreads rapidly throughout the community and beyond. In fact, our Facebook group has members from very diverse locales. One way or another, people hear about us. They repost our videos, and many write encouraging comments on our Facebook and YouTube pages. Such is the power and magic of new media that we worry just a bit less about threats to Americans' first amendment rights to free speech caused by the high costs of advertising and the ever-increasing degree of media consolidation, the very reasons I first proposed this project idea. In fact, one of my class's early videos was in support of a US congressional candidate whose campaign funds were dwarfed by those of his incumbent rival.

Just as important as disseminating a clear political message, however, is the second level, in which we encourage children and teens to get involved and to participate as equals. To become our teachers. To give us their point of view. It is rare in our normally top-down education system for students to have a say in the curricular agenda in this way, so right away we see a benefit. We also believe that the concise form of narration demanded by the mini-film format embodies critical thinking skills, which we think are very useful to a child's education. We further believe that storytelling inculcates skills that a strictly "facts-based" pedagogy does not. And many of our teaching colleagues in our local schools agree. Our project has now become their project.

One can easily see the impact the project has on these children's perspectives. Filmmaking develops a wide variety of academic and social skills. It encourages kids to be concise and creative. The accuracy required by the imposition of the 90-second time constraint forces storytellers to thoroughly understand their topic and ensures that all of the producers do a bit of research in writing their scripts. Kids turn to library and Internet sources and maybe even conduct an interview. Since identifying a social problem and presenting it didactically already implies a solution, we believe that participation in Causes augments the skill of problem solving at a precocious stage of development among children in our public schools. Last, the project promotes teamwork. Many of the filmmakers work in teams. Some of our videos have featured grim statistics on teen pregnancy, local school dropout rates, bullying, and incidences of domestic violence. Storytelling changes the educational dynamic in a most interesting way. When students get to tell the story, they become invested in telling it well. They really do their homework, and they pay attention to the finer details. They also retain information better. In the process, I would argue, they learn more about the topic and something about citizenship as well. All of these positive aspects of Causes were evident to the local donors who have funded the small Causes budget for the past two years.

Perhaps no video better illustrates all of the foregoing arguments than the one entitled *Dear Valdosta City Council*, which was made by a third grade class in 2009 (http://www.youtube.com/watch?v=3Mnz5teLOcA).

So, each year in January, on the Saturday evening between Martin Luther King's Birthday and the Super Bowl, we gather the community and show our films, and we learn together. Interested readers may view the films at our Causes—Valdosta's Mini-Film Festival Facebook group page here: ftp://www.facebook.com/?sk=messages#!/group.php?gid=5717816447&ref=ts. The film festival lasts about two and a half hours, and the atmosphere in the auditorium has a decidedly boisterous feel to it. We encourage this by playing 1960s-era revolutionary pop songs beforehand as well as providing an intermission show featuring a campus improvisational comedy troupe that performs theme-appropriate skits. In short, for a small southern town in the middle of winter, the atmosphere is rarefied. Sometimes amusing, sometimes solemn, there is laughter and there are tears, sharing and empathy.

One other regular feature of our ritual is the distribution of reusable shopping bags to members of the audience, purchased with part of our grant money. My students and I joke that we're igniting revolution right there in the auditorium. And, in fact, recycling and the use of plastic shopping bags and other environmental issues are popular issues at the film festival (see http://www.youtube.com/ watch? v=OA7d5-yaFos). At the same time, however, some of our participants' perspectives are not always what one might call "liberal" or "progressive." We've had interesting takes on the death penalty and pro-life causes over the past few years. But that's okay, too, for there is no more suitable setting for the civil exchange of ideas than a college campus. Moreover, despite our disagreement with some of the issues, we would never wish to do anything to foster censorship. Perhaps due to this philosophy, Causes Film Festival is thriving. We have grown, both in the number of films we've received—from 40 to 65 to 80 over the past three years—as well as in the diversity of our participants. In addition to the participation of some of the local schools, last year's (2009) contributors included a church youth group and a group of breast cancer survivors from upstate New York. Our campus is also well represented, with films being made across the various colleges on campus. In fact, our most watched film so far (73,000 hits on YouTube) is by a physics major, promoting nano-solar technology as a solution to the world's energy problems (see http:// www.youtube.com/watch?v=mCLwk 7ObEr0). Another of our films, produced by an artist and executed in a cartoon format, explores the interesting American contradiction between entitlement programs and the ideology of self-reliance. This was featured on the website of the PBS program *Now*. Yet another on blood donation made a stir with the local Red Cross. Do you have a cause? If so, please make your own 90-second mini-documentary and we'll see you in Valdosta the weekend between the Martin Luther King holiday and the Superbowl.

REFERENCES

Borofsky, Rob. 2007. "Public Anthropology (A Personal Perspective)." http://www.publicanthropology.org/Defining/publicanth-07Oct10.htm.

Richard, Matthew J. 2002. "A Chorus of Fear." http://video.google.com/videoplay?docid=3930808120854021155#.

PART III
Ethnography

Searching for the Spirit: Researching Spirit-Filled Religion in Guatemala

C. Mathews Samson

There are two frames for making sense of the research on Pentecostal religious forms discussed in this essay.[1] First, there has been a significant change in the religious landscape of Latin America over the past 50 years. The most visible evidence of this change is the presence—manifested to the observing eye in the ubiquitous small church buildings (templos) in small towns and megacities throughout the region—of some 15 percent of the population in the ranks of religious communities considered to be Protestant, or *evangelical*, to use the more common term of self-identification among adherents in the region (Steigenga and Cleary 2007, 3).[2] This presence reflects a distinct religious pluralism and a move away from what some have called a monolithic or even a monopolistic Catholicism growing out of the colonial period and through the first 150 years of independence of most of the region from European colonialism (Chesnut 2003). The stages in the shift (both on the ground and in context of more complex academic explications of the culture of the region) have been well documented over last four decades: the advent of liberationist Catholicism, especially in the form of base ecclesial communities following Vatican II; an increasing recognition of the extant religious pluralism in the region, including Afro-Caribbean or Afro-Brazilian religious expressions; a clearer acknowledgment of a persistent indigenous religiosity that has been part of ethnic renewal

movements as indigenous peoples have organized for recognition
and collective rights in the face of social political systems that have
marginalized their voices in the wake of the often-referenced 500
years of conquest; and, most recently, a growing Protestant presence
that is perhaps 75 to 80 percent Pentecostal on a continental scale.
Moreover, the trajectories of these various movements sometimes
embody uneven syncretisms between the traditions, and already in
the late 1980s, we could find the publication of books such as that by
the Mexican American priest, Virgil Elizondo (1988), which, regardless of shortcomings in a strict anthropological sense, proclaimed
that in the Americas *The Future Is Mestizo*.

Second, while keeping this move toward religious pluralism in
the Americas in view, it is also necessary to continue to reframe understandings of world Christianity as a movement and to consider
how global changes are impinging upon particular cases such as
Guatemala and the larger Mesoamerican region, where I have been
working largely on historical Protestantism for nearly a decade and
a half (Samson 2007). Primary in this regard is the shift in the center of gravity of Christianity from the global North and West to
the global South (Jenkins 2002). The immediate implication of this
change is that the majority of Christian adherents in the world at the
beginning of the twenty-first century were to be found in the former
colonized lands of Asia, Africa, and Latin America. In many ways, it
is this shift that will guide the social scientific approaches to Christian pluralism—or even Christianities—in the future.

Less noted until the 1990s in an academic world still wrestling
with the persistence of religion in light of the demise of the secu-
larization thesis that has predicted the end of religion and the death
of God in the face of the inexorable forces of modernity was the
phenomenal growth of the Pentecostal and charismatic wings of
the Christian movement.[3] Sometimes lumped together under the

category of "renewalists," (Pew Forum 2006), Pentecostals and charismatics today account for some 25 percent of the roughly two billion Christians worldwide. Moreover, this is the fastest growing segment of Christianity, and perhaps the fasting growing religious movement in the world. Obviously, its influence will be marked at the global scale over at least the next several decades.

All this is background to the discussion of rather more concise questions. Although as an anthropologist my aim in the study of religious change is to focus on practice elucidated from an ethnographic perspective, here I am concerned initially with the questions of *who* Pentecostals are in Guatemala and *how* it is that they are being Pentecostal in the present moment. My frame for thinking about religion in general and Pentecostalism in particular resonates with the framework suggested by Bruce Lincoln (2003) in his work *Holy Terrors: Thinking about Religion after September 11.* For Lincoln, definitions of religion should be "polythetic and flexible" (4), even as they attend to the arenas of "discourse, practice, community and institution" (7).[4] While I will not deal with each of these aspects here, Lincoln's concerns do provide the texture for a more holistic approach to the study of religion both through time and in particular places. For the purposes of my current research, practice is situated alongside theology and institutional structures in the effort to look at how Pentecostalism as a movement articulates with the larger Guatemalan social context even while projecting the Pentecostal experience into the cultural mainstream and simultaneously working to construct a less sectarian identity as Pentecostals themselves.

FINDING A RESEARCH AGENDA—RELIGIOUS CHANGE IN GUATEMALA IN THE TWENTY-FIRST CENTURY

Beyond the global scene, Guatemala remains a unique—and, in some ways, an astounding case study for considering the problems, pitfalls, and potentialities of applying ethnographic methods to movements such as Protestantism and Pentecostalism. By 1960, after some 80 years of formal missionary presence in the country, Protestantism accounted for what by missionary standards was a rather anemic five percent of the population (Gooren 2001, 183). Beginning in the latter part of the 1960s, the movement began to expand rather rapidly, spurred at times by natural disaster and later by the ongoing revolutionary conflict that began in 1960 and continued until a formal cease-fire was signed in 1996, following the death of some 200,000 and the displacement of a million to a million-and-a-half Guatemalans, either internally within the country or in exile beyond its borders. By the early 2000s, a colleague who has worked in Guatemala for some 30 years remarked that the growth of evangelical churches reflected "the amoeba school of church growth." By the time the Pew Forum conducted its 2006 survey in Guatemala, the country was said to be 34 percent Protestant. This represented a sea change in growth, one that also saw adherence to Catholicism decrease to 48 percent and the rise in people claiming no affiliation to 15 percent. More stunning still, the report also claims that some 60 percent of the entire Guatemalan populace can potentially be categorized as renewalists: 62 percent of Catholics and 85 percent of the Protestants (Pew Forum 2006, 80).

Figure 8.1. Highland Regions of Guatemala. Map by Dr. James Samson.

The implications of this change are only beginning to be understood, and one can argue that despite considerable research in the
area we are still defining the questions. Research, to some degree,
is not only targeted but also serendipitous, in the sense that "being
there" is impacted by the events taking place at the moment one
happens to be in the field, especially on short-term research trips.
Religion makes news all the time in Guatemala, and I got a particular take on contrasting perspectives regarding how evangelical, specifically Pentecostal, preoccupations continue to make themselves
known in the discourses of civil society in contemporary Guatemala.

The most prominent form of Pentecostal discourse is that of neo-
Pentecostalism embodied in elite-based religion, such as that ema-
nating from Guatemala City's megachurches like the Fraternidad
Cristiana with its new 12,500 seat sanctuary, the Megafrater, or the
El Shaddai congregation and its pastor Harold Caballeros, famous

for his doctrine of spiritual warfare and the slogan "Jesús Es Señor de Guatemala" ("Jesus is Lord of Guatemala"). At the same time, there remains a tie in the discourse and the existence of these congregations to the presence of General Efraín Ríos Montt, dictator and president of the country during one of the bloodiest periods of the civil war. Embedded in the narratives constructed by these groups is an emphasis on God's sovereignty and control over human affairs, as well as a notion that the evangelical vision is one that should be used for governance. An article that appeared in Guatemala's leading daily newspaper, *Prensa Libre*, the day I went back into the field in 2009 took a look at the religious commitments of members of the Guatemalan congress. Several pieces of information were interesting and worthy of further reflection, but particularly striking was the notion that the party Ríos Montt founded, the *Frente Republicano Guatemalteco* (FRG), continues to have the highest percentage of evangelicals in its ranks (*filas*). Beyond this density, one of the party leaders proudly proclaimed in the article that "'the Bible is one of the manuals that [we] use and follow in order to govern'" (Marroquín and Cardona 2009, 12).[5]

This language was striking enough, but a week later an op-ed appeared in the same paper; it was written by the Maya indigenous activist Sam Colop (2009) and reported on yet another effort to form an evangelical political party—or at least one founded on biblical principles, if not strictly evangelical in its definition. There Colop cites a report in another daily (*La Hora*, 27 May 2009) where a current leader of the FRG essentially put an exclamation point on the statement above by saying, "Christianity is always present in all the political and ideological aspects of the FRG." The FRG leader in this case was identified as Nicolás de León, who "says that the Bible is the manual of his party." After labeling de León a hypocrite because of his connection with the FRG, Colop quotes him again, "'If God gives us life, then man cannot take it away.'" For those accustomed to the continuing debate over the separation of church and state in the United States, such language is jarring. Nevertheless, the ethnographic stance is first to make sense of what is going on, and when Colop, in the same opinion piece, turns directly to the issue of the new political party, he reports the following comment: "We are not forming a church; we are forming a political group that includes everyone that believes in Jesus Christ."[6]

Several days after this article appeared, I received a more circumspect response regarding how evangelicals might engage with the political arena from the director of an educational institution associated with the Iglesia de Dios del Evangélio Completo (IDEC, Full Gospel Church of God). He responded to a description of my research by making a strong statement that social science research was needed for his own denomination in Guatemala. It was a conversation setting up a further interview, so I only captured the sense of what he was saying: "The culture of violence is affecting us greatly. And what is the church doing?" After mentioning several problems, such as social exclusion and corruption, he then remarked on the necessity of understanding and interpreting such phenomena. He concluded by saying, "We greatly need social scientific study. The church in Guatemala is an experience-based church" ("una iglesia empírica"). In contrast to the neo-Pentecostal vision, he ended with a statement that it is a challenge (reto) to govern but that it is also a challenge for the evangel (el evangélio) to touch and transform social reality.

Coming from the interview context itself, these comments were the equivalent of being handed a research agenda on a silver platter. The framework that begins to take shape from out of the two perspectives recounted involves framing the tension involved in evangelical, particularly Pentecostal, identity and the engagement of

Pentecostalism with civil society in Guatemala, including notions of what one student of neo-Pentecostalism has called "Christian citizenship" (O'Neill 2007). Others have focused more broadly in Latin America and elsewhere on the contributions of evangelicals to processes of democratization (Freston 2001, 2008). Given the crisis of economy and what seems to be endemic violence in Guatemala in the post-conflict era, the Guatemalan case once again becomes one that applies beyond the borders of a relatively small nation-state in a region that is sometimes perceived as a backwater even in Latin America.[7]

Practice, Theology, and Full Gospel Roots

Part of this examination of Pentecostalism requires a closer look at the intersections of religion and society in Guatemala from the religious vantage point. It seems clear that discourse within FRG as a political party and within the neo-Pentecostal community at large continues to promote what Manuela Cantón Delgado has referred to as "biblical-ideological discourse" (Cantón Delgado 1998, 265). This discourse is powerful; it links a kind of biblical faith and political ideology in a single package; and it does influence the practice of other evangelical groups as well, in part through media influence and because its leaders are often sought out by the more traditional politicos who are trying to carve out space for their own agendas. Yet, the intent in my research at this juncture is to shift some of the attention away from the neo-Pentecostals and to look ethnographically at the Pentecostal tradition with all of its own contradictions. Much discourse in the evangelical community refers to how evangelicals can work to *incidir* (influence) or even transform social reality in the country. My sense is that among Pentecostals this has to do less with transforming the political reality than with a grounded sense of connection with place and context. While specific discourses need to be examined on a case-by-case basis, there is also a fundamental difference in the scale of engagement with society at large in the Pentecostal and neo-Pentecostal communities. Some of this has to do with the relative wealth and power within the respective communities, but it is also related to the way in which Pentecostals assume their place in local community contexts throughout the nation.

At the same time, there continues to be a considerable divergence between urban and rural segments of the Guatemalan population, particularly in those rural areas of the western highlands inhabited primarily by the Maya peoples, who speak 22 languages and make up perhaps 55 percent of the nation's population. Within religious groups that have significant numbers of both mestizos and Maya in their ranks, practice varies widely from rural to urban contexts, and looking for commonality in practice is not always as easy as one might hope in trying to construct a linear argument.

The case I am using as the basis for this consideration of Pentecostalism is that of the Full Gospel Church of God (*Iglesia de Dios del Evangélio Completo*, IDEC), the second largest Pentecostal denomination in Guatemala (behind the Assemblies of God). Although the roots of Pentecostalism go as far back as 1910 and the work of Albert Hines in the K'iche' regions of the departments of Totonicapán and El Quiché, for the IDEC, the important early missionaries were Charles Furman and Thomas Pullin, who arrived under the auspices of the United Free Gospel and Missionary Society in 1916.[8] Furman affiliated with the Primitive Methodists in 1922 and left that denomination under duress in 1934 after an outpouring of the Spirit in communities in the area of the department of Totonicapán. The denomination celebrates 1932 as its year of origin in Guatemala in response to the advent of the Spirit.[9] From that beginning, the recent growth of the denomination by most forms of accounting has been phenomenal. Richard Waldrop's (1993, 56) dissertation records some 84,366 members and 1,508 churches in 1990. At the same time, there were 343 missions and 1,601 ministers.[10] By 2009, the numbers had increased to 204,190 members, 2,263 churches, 870 missions, and 3,179 ministers—in membership alone, an increase of approximately 142 percent in two decades.[11]

I can do little more than hint at some of the issues that the Iglesia de Dios responds to in seeking to carry out its mission in the Guatemalan context. In terms of institutional practice, the seminary director mentioned before went to some length to indicate that the denomination has worked with what he said were 22 of the 23 different ethnic groups in the country. Only the Garífuna of the Caribbean coastal region near the city of Livingston are excluded, and some attempts at evangelization had been made among that population. For him, this was evidence of a multicultural and multilingual church that began with cultural values as a fundamental. When I asked about the attitude of the church toward Maya customary ceremonies practiced in places on the natural landscape considered sacred by the Maya, in some ways he could have been giving a discourse on cultural relativism in a class in introductory cultural anthropology. He emphasized that the customary practices had their own meaning and that it was important to understand what their meaning was for the communities themselves. His discourse on syncretism was less amenable to my academic gaze, but he, nevertheless, acknowledged that as the evangelical churches broke with this syncretism (Maya-Catholic) in Maya communities that people were indeed changing the religious practices of their ancestors—on the basis of both Western culture and "the Gospel." In addition, the denomination has tried to work cooperatively with local workers and has tried to resist missionary models of domination, and this has opened space for indigenous leadership within Guatemala.

Minimally, then, there seems to be an awareness in segments of the IDEC educational community that dialogue across cultures is essential in contemporary Guatemala. Investigating how that plays out in various local contexts is one direction for research. Beyond this, however, I had been puzzled in several visits to Pentecostal churches during summer field seasons in 2008 and 2009 at how sedate the services had appeared in contrast to one I attended several years ago when I was involved in a film project—no speaking in tongues, no dancing or falling out in the spirit, and certainly no exorcisms or miraculous healings. When I asked what had happened to the Spirit, I received this answer:

> There has been a great error in identifying Pentecostalism as synonymous with glossolalia.... Pentecostalism has been analyzed in sociological instead of theological terms. As well it has been analyzed as a function of its liturgical phenomenology instead of on the basis of, let's say, its theological legacy.... And I think that it was an error of appreciation that evolved into a prejudice against Pentecostals.... Logically, we as Pentecostals have distinctive doctrinal features.... As the Church of God, we belong to classical or historical Pentecostalism.... And I think that the theological synthesis to be understood is that the sovereignty of God and human freedom are not in contradiction. Rather, the Christian faith is obligated, in a certain way, not to make a caricature of God, but neither to create a caricature of the human being.... For us Pentecostals, baptism with the Holy Spirit doesn't have a soteriological root. We don't relate it to the work of salvation; instead we relate baptism, doctrine, and the experience of baptism with the Holy Spirit with the mission of the church. And that which is distinctive about baptism with the Holy Spirit, which logically cannot be

reduced to glossolalia, is fundamentally a life of obedi-
ence to God and a high commitment to the mission of
God in the world.

I felt in the end that I had received a lesson in Wesleyan and Ar-
minian theology as payment for that particular interview.

Beyond Pluralism in the Study of Guatemalan Religious Change

Addressing the complex of issues related to inequality in Latin America alongside a parallel agenda directed toward understanding religious change requires a look beyond the phenomenon of evangelical
growth and rupture of the religious monopoly of Catholicism in the
region. One aspect of this is the need to continue the ethnographic
approach to theory and practice in order to analyze how Pentecostals are actually responding to inequality and other forms of social
injustice as their numbers continue to grow. As I indicated at the
beginning of this essay, the framing of such an agenda points to both
scholarly and practical realities in the study of religious change in
Latin America. An explication of the use of the Bible as a guide for
governance, regardless of which place one occupies on the political
spectrum, within a political party that maintains its roots among the
nation's elite is not the most direct route to understanding Pentecostal attempts at citizenship and participation in society.

While it might be fair to suggest that issues of citizenship and
democratization as such are not on the forefront of the minds of
most evangelicals, perhaps especially Pentecostals, it is significant
that some Pentecostals themselves are raising the question—not
only of what it means to be a Pentecostal in a violent and unequal
social milieu but of what the broader evangelical community has
to contribute to the society writ large. Some of this can be seen in
the emphasis on mission as opposed to soteriology, salvation, in the

seminary director's comments. Now two decades removed from the preoccupation about whether Latin America would turn Protestant (Stoll 1990), the question may now be how Protestants of all stripes are turning Latin American and responding to their own context by projecting their own reality outward toward their own societies. This is in many ways the perspective of grounded ethnography that seeks the "insider's point of view" in regard to "how" people are Pentecostal, but it is also an agenda that requires a continued interdisciplinary approach to understanding, including the incorporation of some understanding of how theological perspectives intersect with practical concerns in the process of defining the identity of self and community.

One aspect of such an approach is to consider both the theology and the institutionalization process of a denomination like the IDEC in Guatemala. As part of a larger ecclesial structure that transcends denominational definitions based on international boundaries, the church claims to be self-supporting within Guatemala, while some of the historical denominations, notably the Presbyterians, continue to depend on a shrinking largesse from a mother or sister denomination. Moreover, reflection on the historical trajectory of the denomination, despite its missionary past, reveals a preoccupation with a "cooperative" type of ministry from the beginning. This effort to establish an autochthonous identity is ingrained in the place of Guatemala. In turn, such rootedness provides a freedom of practice that allows particular congregations and individuals to embrace their own realities in radically different cultural contexts: urban, middle-class Mestizo or predominately rural Maya, as well as people moving between and beyond such static definitions of identity.

Here, the Pentecostal experience provides a point of reference that promises to relativize our understandings of evangelical reality throughout the Americas. Even among theologians, particularly those of a more progressive persuasion, there is talk of an evangelical subculture that distinguishes itself by a limited discourse that can be seen, according to José Duque of the Latin American Biblical University, in events such as "the 'Great march for the protection of marriage, the family, and social peace'" that was held in San José, Costa Rica, in July of 2008. Duque is not an anthropologist, so he combines a theological viewpoint that takes evangelicals and the evangelical community as an object, one in which he presumably has some investment. His views on the issues are not, I suspect, so different from those of many academics who continue to try to make sense of the sea change in Latin America's religious landscape.

In this evangelical subculture, a centrist model has been constructed with authoritarian objectives—individualistic in order to massify and magical in order to mystify....In this subculture, the community of believers has no other purpose than to provide financial resources to sustain the extravagant desires and habits of those privileged leaders. These are leaders who self-proclaim themselves "apostles" and "prophets," and as such, they are converted into absolute masters because they have no other authority than that which they themselves establish. For them, the only problem that humanity has suffered since forever is that of finances. Following this premise, injustice, corruption, violence, exclusion, unemployment, and even poverty are magically resolved with healthy finances (Duque 2008).

Duque continues by asking some pointed questions about how academic theologians and others with a preoccupation for the evangelical community will respond to the current situation: "What are the socio-economic and religious conditions of our regional context that make possible not only the protagonism of such an evangelical leadership but also the preoccupying existence of a massified religious base that consumes superficiality, emotionalism, individualism, and magical utilitarian automatism?" Beyond religion, the argument is that other disciplines are needed to answer this question. He calls it a transdisciplinary concern because "utilitarian massification is also occurring in political contexts and show business (*farándula*)."

Anthropologically, the more important view might be one that begins with practice but also looks toward the way in which evangelical culture responds to contemporary concerns, including violence and injustice. Because of their apparent numerical superiority, it seems logical to say that the center of gravity within the evangelical community resides within the Pentecostal segment.[12] While diverse in and of itself, a concerted effort by social scientists directed toward understanding Pentecostal discourse and practice might lead to a clearer picture of the nature of the Pentecostal contribution to the communities where they are present. In the face of the profound social inequalities in Central America, in particular, it may be time to ask if evangelicals are really a subculture in greater Mesoamerica after all. Rather they are citizens seeking to make their mark on a world that is indeed filled with demons—poverty, violence, political insensitivity to the masses, racism, femicide.

Beyond, or perhaps beneath, the neo-Pentecostal discourse that speaks of governing with the Bible in hand, the Pentecostals present a different kind of vision; they may in the end not be as sectarian or otherworldly as those from other religious or academic traditions have assumed. While I am not quite ready to label either evangelicals or Pentecostals as harbingers of a social movement, there are certainly elements of social movement mobilization involved in their activities, and a more fruitful approach is to think of Pentecostals as mediators in social networks and potential creators of social capital that will bridge a narrow evangelical identity and inhere in society in ways that are yet to be determined. In the words of Daniel Chiquete, "By their very nature the Pentecostalisms are natural promoters of plurality and inter-cultural [sic] contact. They have the capacity to

build bridges between different cultural worlds. And their alternative vision and experience reject and restrict any ideology that sets
out to be all-encompassing" (Chiquete 2002, 36).[13]

CONCLUSION: ENGAGING THE SPIRIT IN A CHANGING
LANDSCAPE

I conclude with two other experiences and a propaganda piece from
a regional conference of leaders I stumbled upon when I went to
meet an IDEC pastor and travel with him to his community for an
interview. He is a Mam Maya pastor who lives in the municipality
of San Juan Ostuncalco in an *aldea* (village) that is 95 percent indigenous. I met him at a meeting in an urban church building that
has occupied a prominent place in the regional commercial center of
Quetzaltenango, traditionally considered Guatemala's second city in
both economic and cultural terms. When I arrived at the church, a
meeting was in process that included both Maya and Mestizo leaders from throughout the district around Quetzaltenango, and I witnessed about an hour of the meeting as leaders, mostly ministers
including a small number of women, were exhorted to preoccupy
themselves with mission and to promote the unity of their church—
una sola iglesia—because it is *la* iglesia de dios, *the* Church of God.
Members were encouraged to take home posters with a large eye
peering back at the viewer. The pupil in the eye was an image of the
world with clouds above it, and the eye was placed over a statement
that was simply titled "*Visión*":

> We desire to be a Church
> full of the Holy Spirit, in constant growth,
> of thousands and thousands of Christians that congregate
> to worship God in spirit and in truth,
> that has a profound passion for the lost

and a commitment with world missions,

discipleship, the establishment of new churches,

and that knows how to extend its hands to help those who suffer.

This is a vision of what they might call the full or complete Gospel, and it is rooted in a sense of community that extends to the ends of the earth. I had been struck a few days before by the Pentecostal sense of encompassing geography when I had attended a service led by the same Mam minister. He preached on what might be called the prologue to Pentecost, when the risen Jesus at the beginning of the Acts of the Apostles directs the gathered apostles to wait for the Spirit, at which time they would become witnesses in Jerusalem, in Judea, and on into Samaria and the ends of the earth (Acts 1:7-8). This was a service not like the one I had attended in the city the year before, when I had been handed a bulletin filled with congregational activity information on the way in, and where a praise band had opened the service with songs, pictures, and where even a video for the pastor's sermon was projected onto a screen so that everyone could participate. Here, at least on the evening I attended, the warm-up music, which is actually a large component of the service, was done a cappella, and the prayers (which I was assured were not speaking in tongues) had most of the congregation on their knees in front of plastic chairs while everyone prayed aloud in a manner so that a whistling tone pervaded the small *templo*.

Although singing and Bible reading are done in Spanish, most of the preaching was tied to Mam, with some Spanish interpolations thrown in. When the minister addressed the situation of the apostles in Acts, he painted for the congregation a cognitive geographic map that led from Jerusalem—the area of the local congregation—to Judea—Guatemala the nation—to Samaria. In his own way, he described as a transcultural space—a place where one had to interact with ladinos, or mestizos, in a broader context on the way to the evangelization of the world. I had not felt the spirit, but it was powerful approach to a text about the presence of the Spirit being with the disciples even as they went out to the ends of the world. Of course, I could not be sure how the congregants heard this proclamation, but in the post-conflict situation where violence and discrimination are not experiences of the past, and in a place where continuing migratory patterns lead from mountain communities throughout Guatemala to El Norte, it was a powerful invocation of work and context. As the evangelical might say, it was a new Word, and a somewhat unexpected one, even after all these years, as I watched many of the women, without exception in the customary dress of the Mam, bring leaves for wrapping tamales and lay them on the raised chancel area as a *primicía* or first fruit offering, the leaves of the corn plant actually representing the first fruit rather than the maize itself.

I again experienced this sense of religiosity being projected beyond a particular place—or at least beyond a particular worldview, surely in part a function of the religious imaginary, a couple of weeks later when I accompanied one of the congregation members to a Maya altar or ceremonial site high on a hilltop overlooking the village and learned that it was place of special significance where sometimes all the Maya spiritual guides (shamans) in the community gathered for ceremonies, frequently to ask together for rain for the *milpa* (cornfields) at the beginning of May and to give thanks if the rains had already begun to fall. He then pointed to an adjacent space covered with leaves where the evangelicals sometimes climbed the mountain for fasting, vigils, and prayers—also to ask for blessing and to give thanks. The religious landscape in Guatemala today is one where sacred space is both shared and negotiated.

Photograph 8.1. Mayan ceremonial site.

In conducting this type of research, ethnographic distance is often challenged both by what people think and how they respond to the experience of the Spirit. When I conducted a focus group with some 20 ministers and lay people at the IDEC seminary in Guatemala City, my presence and interest in the lives of the group members was appreciated. At the same time, I was at one point put into a corner when I asked about experiences people had had with healings, and one minister decided to ask me if I believed the stories they were sharing. I remember thinking briefly that perhaps I had no business doing this kind of research, that in a strange sort of way I had gotten in over my head—not because I was about to go native by speaking in tongues, which in any case would go against my own rather stiff Presbyterian roots, but because I could only respond by saying that what I believed wasn't the issue. Rather what I was concerned with was the particular experiences of those who were willing to share.

These were stories of an encounter with the Spirit that seems not to be open to me in either an ethnographic or a spiritual sense. Nevertheless, I was moved when I asked participants to share something of the first time they experienced an encounter with the Spirit. One middle-aged man began to cry and then became speechless. Out of respect, no one in the room moved as he collected his thoughts and searched for words to describe what to the outsider is indescribable. I approached and put my hand on his shoulder until he finished his story—providing an ending I cannot even remember. Later I engaged one of my colleagues, herself a Pentecostal of the same denomination, with a comment about how meaningful it was to have people share their experiences with me and how moving it was to watch their reactions to the memory of these profound and personal encounters with the Spirit. She responded by saying that the experience "is so emotional that people guard it within themselves. They keep it like a death; it is never repeated."

The ethnographic stance is one in which the ethnographic lens becomes a bridge between one culture and another, sometimes serving as a bridge for cross-cultural, and even intercultural understanding. And we can be sure that Pentecostals in Guatemala will continue to see the moving of the Spirit in places were some of us see only conflict and contradiction.

NOTES

1. A version of this essay was first presented at the XVIII Congress of the Latin American Studies Association in Rio de Janeiro, Brazil, in June of 2009. It was revised for presentation at the Southern Anthropological Society meeting in Savannah, Georgia, in February of 2010.

2. This figure should be taken as indication of the magnitude of the shift and not as a hard and fast number. In using such percentages for Protestant demographics, I try to maintain a position in the conservative to middle range of those currently available. Steigenga (2010) posits a reconceptualization of the significance of conversion, based on both experience and the literature about conversion in Latin America. Say the number is even higher.

3. Pentecostalism was not ignored by any stretch of the imagination, but its force was not widely acknowledged the way it is two decades later. See David Martin's *Tongues of Fire: The Explosion of Protestantism in Latin America* (1990) and Harvey Cox's *Fire from Heaven* (1995).

4. For more on this ethnographic perspective and other directions for research in regard to Pentecostalism, see also Steigenga (2001, 152-155).

5. Translations from Spanish sources are my own.

6. The party was to be called Victoria, and it would be led by Abraham Rivera, the well-known former alcalde of Mixco, a contiguous suburb of Guatemala City and perhaps the country's second largest city in terms of actual population.

7. For O'Neill, it is a discourse that puts the "weight" of changing the nation on the individual believer. This clearly puts the concern on the believer and believer's community for taking responsibility for making changes in society, but it skirts the question of how neo-Pentecostal discourse seems limited in its ability to address issues of structural change in a society battered by violence and economic distress.

8. The details about Hines are from Smith (2006). Smith relies in part on a Spanish language document that I have not seen, written by Richard Waldrop, who was a Church of God missionary in Guatemala for a number of years and now teaches at the Church of God seminary in Cleveland, Tennessee. For more details on this early history, see Garrard-Burnett (1998, 37-38, and 2001).

9. Waldrop (1993, 23-28) discusses Furman's relationship to the Primitive Methodists at length, emphasizing that Furman was always forthcoming about his Pentecostal identity throughout his relationship with them. Garrard-Burnett (1998, 39) provides a chart showing that by 1935, the IDEC counted some 17 congregations and that six of these were pastored by men with indigenous surnames. This reflects both the extent of the Pentecostal network in that time period as well as the way in which Pentecostalism became rooted in some indigenous communities from an early date.

10. The exact meaning of the latter category is unclear. There is a single ordination in the denomination, but various tasks are fulfilled by those ordained. The meaning of ordination and, therefore, hierarchy in leadership still needs to be clarified in this study.

11. These numbers come from the denomination's monthly report and are "actualized" as of 1 June 2009. I am using the figure listed for monthly membership. A category reporting past membership (*membresia pasada*) lists the membership for an earlier date at 223,404. The person who provided the numbers was not clear on the difference, but he said that there was a concern within the IDEC for membership inflation in the tracking provided in these statistics.

12. It is significant that the president of the Alianza Evangélica in 2009 was a member of the IDEC. While the Alianza has a reputation

for a conservative theological and political agenda, it was founded as a specifically ecumenical institution, largely by Guatemala's "historical" denominations. It will be interesting to note the trajectory in the future.

13. See Levine (2009) for a discussion of religious pluralism on a continental scale in Latin America. MacKenzie (2005) has significant discussions of both Catholic and Pentecostal practices in a K'iche' Maya community not far from where I conducted my research.

REFERENCES

Cabanas, Andrés. 2009. "Guatemala: Dos países. Revolución, 22 de Febrero." http://www.rebelion.org/noticia.php?id=81260.

Cantón Delgado, Manuela. 1998. "Bautizados en fuego: Protestantes, discursos de conversión y política en Guatemala (1989-1993)." La Antigua, Guatemala South. Woodstock, Vermont: CIRMA and Plumsock Mesoamerican Studies.

Chesnut, R. Andrew. 2003. *Competitive Spirits: Latin America's New Religious Economy*. New York: Oxford University Press.

Chiquete, Daniel. 2002. "Latin American Pentecostalisms and Western Postmodernism: Reflections on a Complex Relationship." *International Review of Mission* 92(364):29-39.

Cleary, Edward L. 2004. "Shopping Around: Questions about Latin American Conversions." *International Bulletin of Missionary Research* 28(2):50-54.

Colop, Sam. 2009. "Dios y los políticos, (Ucha'xik)," *Prensa Libre* 30 de Mayo, 16.

Duque, José. 2008. "Un fenómeno que reta la educación teológica." *Rectoral* (Universidad Bíblica Latinoamericana), Mayo-Agosto, 2.

Elizondo, Virgilio P. 1988. *The Future is Mestizo: Life Where Cultures Meet*. Oak Park, IL: Meyer-Stone Books.

Freston, Paul. 2001. *Evangelicals and Politics in Asia, Africa, and Latin America*. Cambridge: Cambridge University Press.

————., ed. 2008. *Evangelical Christianity and Democracy in Latin America*. New York: Oxford University Press.

Garrard-Burnett, Virginia. 1998. *Living in the New Jerusalem: Protestantism in Guatemala*. Austin: University of Texas Press.

————. 2001. "Tongues, People, and Convolutionists: Early Pentecostalism in Guatemala, 1914-1940." Paper presented at the XIII International Congress of the Latin American Studies Association, Washington, D.C.

Gooren, Henri. 2001. "Reconsidering Protestant Growth in Guatemala." In *Holy Saints and Fiery Preachers: The Anthropology of Protestantism in Mexico and Central America*, edited by James W. Dow and Alan R. Sandstrom, 169-203. Westport, Connecticut: Praeger.

Jenkins, Philip. 2002. *The Next Christendom: The Coming of Global Christianity*. New York: Oxford University Press.

Levine, Daniel H. 2009. "The Future of Christianity in Latin America." *Journal of Latin American Studies* 41:121-145.

Lincoln, Bruce. 2003. *Holy Terrors: Thinking about Religion after September 11*. Chicago and London: University of Chicago Press.

MacKenzie, Christopher James. 2005. "Maya Bodies and Minds: Religion and Modernity in a K'iche' Town." Ph.D. diss., University at Albany, State University of New York.

Marroquín, M., M. Fernández, and K. Cardona. 2009. "Un congreso con equilibrio espiritual." *Prensa Libre* 24 de Mayo, 12-13.

O'Neill, Kevin Lewis. 2007. "City of God: Neo-Pentecostal
    Formations of Christian Citizenship in Postwar Guatemala."
    Ph.D. diss., Stanford University.

Pew Forum on Religion and Public Life. 2006. "Spirit and Power:
    A 10-Country Survey of Pentecostals." Washington, D.C.
    http://pewforum.org/newassets/surveys/Pentecostal/
    Pentecostals-08.pdf.

Samson, C. Mathews. 2007. *Re-enchanting the World: Maya
    Protestantism in the Guatemalan Highlands*. Tuscaloosa:
    University of Alabama Press.

_____. 2008. "From War to Reconciliation: Guatemalan
    Evangelicals and the Transition to Democracy, 1982-2001."
    In *Evangelical Christianity and Democracy in Latin America*,
    edited by Paul Freston, 63-96. New York: Oxford University
    Press.

Smith, Dennis. 2006. "Los teleapóstoles guatemaltecos: Apuntes
    históricos y propuestas para la investigación." Paper
    presented at the XXVI Congress of the Latin American
    Studies Association. 15-19 March. San Juan, Puerto Rico.

Steigenga, Timothy J. 2001. "The Politics of the Spirit: The Political
    Implications of Pentecostalized Religion in Costa Rica and
    Guatemala." Lanham, MD: Lexington Books.

_____. 2010. "Religious Conversion in the Americas: Meaning,
    Measures, and Methods." *International Bulletin of Missionary
    Research* 34(2):77-82.

_____, and Edward L. Cleary. 2007. "Understanding Conversion
    in the Americas." In *Conversion of a Continent:
    Contemporary Religious Change in Latin America*, edited by
    T. J. Steigenga and Edward L. Cleary, 3-32. New
    Brunswick, NJ: Rutgers University Press.

Stoll, David. 1990. *Is Latin America Turning Protestant?* Berkeley: University of California Press.

Waldrop, Richard E. 1993. "An Historical and Critical Review of the Full Gospel Church of God of Guatemala." D. Miss. diss., Fuller Theological Seminary.

"Ooo Ooo, Aah Aah": People, Bonobos, and Mirrored Projections at the Zoo

Robert Shanafelt

This paper is a preliminary discussion of findings based on observations made at the Jacksonville Zoo and Gardens in 2009 and 2010. *Ethnoprimatology* and the synonym *cultural primatology* are names first suggested in the 1990s for the study of human primate relationships and how humans conceive of those relationships (Sponsel 1997; Wheatley 1999). Key texts in the field by anthropologists include Ohnuki-Tierney (1987), Peterson and Goodall (2000), Fuentes and Wolfe (2002), and Corbey (2005). The work of Ramona and Desmond Morris (1966) needs also to be mentioned as a pioneering work as does that of Donna Haraway (1989), the latter being a seminal text in critical historical analysis of primatology as a scientific endeavor.

My interest lies in how ordinary people perceive great apes, most particularly bonobos. I present here examples of some of the common motifs people express as they describe bonobo actions and appearances. I organize these into two broad types. First are those I label Mirrored Behavioral Analogies (MBAs) because they seem to involve one-to-one correspondences between bonobo actions and human actions. Second are those I call Misconceived Interpretive Schemas (MISes). While both involve the human observer in drawing parallels between bonobo actions and human cultural models and linguistic frames, in the MISes, there is activation of an interpretive frame that leads to significant misperception. The "ooo-ooo aah aah" of the title is one example of a MIS, in that observers, in making this vocalization as they encounter bonobos, project their expectations of chimpanzee vocalizations onto bonobos, and then afterwards often do not even notice that these do not fit. The Jacksonville Zoo and Gardens is home to some 275 species of animals, with approximately 1,400 individuals. Besides bonobos, the zoo has a number of other primates, including ring-tailed and black-and-white ruffed lemurs, colobus monkeys, squirrel monkeys, siamangs, mandrills, and Western lowland gorillas. At the time of my research there were 11 bonobos, with 3 adult males, and 8 females of various ages. Lorel was the eldest of the group (b. 1969), a mother of seven, with four offspring still in the zoo with her.[1] Lorel's offspring ranged in ages from 6 to 26 and included three daughters and a son. Lorel's first child was the famous language-trained Kanzi. He avoided zoo life after he was taken away by another bonobo female, Matata. The second eldest female in the group was Kuni, born in 1985. She has had three offspring, but only her young infant (born November 2009) was with her. The third eldest female Lori (b. 1987) was a mother of two, aged 8 and 13. The preferred breeding male was Akili, 29.

Visitors to the bonobo area of the zoo never see all 11 bonobos together, because only a subset are outside at any given time. On many of the occasions I visited, there were all female groups out, sometimes even all of them together. Males were let out less frequently, generally as a single male in combination with females to whom they are compatible. There is no public access to the inside caged-areas where the bonobos are kept.

It is not controversial to suggest that people can easily identify with animals, but I would like to add some specificity to that generalization. My observations of "people watching apes at the zoo" have led me to believe that our tendencies to project intentionality onto others, even onto inanimate objects, is heightened by an unconscious mapping that goes on between human and bonobo morphology and actions. Recent work on primate mirror neuron systems would suggest that when an ape jumps, swings, climbs, puts a hand out, or moves in other ways that are second nature to us, we may experience this movement psychologically as if we ourselves were making that movement. As one of the pioneers in this research has noted, "Neither the monkey nor the human can observe someone else picking up an apple [for example] without also invoking in the brain the motor plans necessary to snatch that apple themselves" (Iacoboni 2008, 14). In other words, when we see someone doing something that we know how to do, a part of our brain is activated as if we ourselves were doing it. And, it is not at all farfetched to make the claim that this can happen when humans watch apes, since it was observation of monkeys watching humans pick up things that led to the discovery in the first place! In fact, knowledge that such systems exist first came to be realized after brain researchers who had planted electrodes in a part of a macaque's brain [F5 in premotor cortex] noticed that specific neurons fired when the macaque watched a human pick up an object.

What I call Mirrored Behavioral Analogies (MBAs) are given this name because I believe they are grounded in such mirror-neuron activation. If this does indeed occur, the system would be automatic and outside of volitional control. However, activation of a human's mirror neurons while watching an ape do something would not necessarily foster self-reflective analysis or lead to a conscious sense of human-animal kinship. (In fact, it might lead to feelings of disgust.) I would maintain, though, that it is likely to foster relevant vocal commentary, especially when several people are together watching the bonobos. While I obviously cannot say what is going on in people's brains when they're at the zoo, I can say that when human children and adults enter into "co-presence" with bonobos there, they frequently make spontaneous comments that express direct links between human and ape appearances, behaviors, and intentions. At the very least, this suggests that the animals are being thought of in some way as one with humans, regardless of what those who express the comments may feel about our taxonomic or evolutionary relationships.

TYPES OF ANALOGIES AND SCHEMAS

Let me now give some examples of what I mean by MBAs and of what I believe follows from them at a more conscious level, direct connection to familiar action schemas. The first examples draw on what seem to me to be very basic analogies:

Analogies

"Look, they're hugging" (Fieldnotes 10/10/2009)

"Look they're holding hands"...

"... Chasing ... wee" ... (Fieldnotes 9/5/2009)

"Looks like they're playing a little game"... (Fieldnotes 9/5/2009)

"They're all cuddling together." ..."They're wrestling."

"Look at the piggy back ride." (Fieldnotes 1/17/2010)

Such comments appear spontaneous, are frequent, and are typical. They are said in similar ways by individuals who, as far as I can tell, do not know one another and who often appear to be seeing bonobos for the first time. They derive from people's experience with each other, not with apes, and not from their expectations of apes. (See Photograph 9.1.)

Photograph 9.1. Piggy back ride. Photograph by Robert Shanafelt.

In fact, if you did not know the context, you would have no way of knowing whether or not the comments were made with respect to people or to bonobos. This is also true of the second set of examples I will provide. The difference here is that with the second set the tone tends toward negative moral evaluation, and the comments may relate to conceptions of nudity and physicality. Evaluation is typically prompted by perceived violations of human rules, ideal body images, or body taboos. (See Photograph 9.2.)

Evaluations

> He's showin' off"... "He's scratchin' his butt" (Fieldnotes 9/5/2009)

> "They've got big (ugly) butts [boodies]" (Comment heard every observation day)

> "He's [Lucy] putting on clothes—finally covering up his butt" [Context: bonobos have been given cloth to play with] (Fieldnotes 8/6/2009)

"Their butts are showin'. They're moonin' us. He's scratchin it too." (Fieldnotes 8/6/2009)

"Eeeeew" [Comment on bonobos urinating, putting fingers in anus, nose, or in genital area]

"That one's picking its nose ... nasty." [1/18/2010] "He's eatin' his boogers." [9/5/10]

Woman (1): "She's got a hand on it" [ha..ha..ha] ... Woman (2): "They're just doin' what comes natural." (11/29/10)

Photograph 9.2. Evaluation: Showing off or overexposure? Photograph by Robert Shanafelt.

Some comments on social-sexual behavior might be placed here too, but many of these comments do not fit so neatly into my contrast between Mirrored Behavioral Analogy and Misconceived Interpretive Schemas; they appear to reflect both. On the one hand, direct analogies with human behavior are drawn; whether they are based on personal sexual experience or merely imagined is another question. On the other hand, there is a mistake in perception when the female-to-female nature of the sexual encounters is not recognized. While it is not clear from the comments alone that the observers were referencing heterosexual behavior, other evidence suggests that this is typically the case. For example, observers typically expressed surprise when it was pointed out to them that what they were witnessing was female-to-female behavior. All of the following comments were made while the speakers were witnessing female-to-female contacts. (See Photograph 9.3.)

Sexual Analogies

> "[That's a] monkey orgy—you can put that on You-Tube!"
>
> "That one put its boody in the other's mouth!"
>
> "He's going down!" ..."You [bonobo] nasty" (Teenager group 8/6/2009)
>
> "Hey, hey, keep it legal around here. This is a family zoo. (10/10/2009)
>
> "Eeeew ..."
>
> "She's doing it [while holding] a baby!" (1/17/10)

Photograph 9.3. G-g rubbing. Photograph by Robert Shanafelt.

Another step removed from the simplest Mirrored Behavioral Analogies are comments that involve drawing more complex parallels between bonobos and humans. They are not merely descriptions or descriptions with evaluative remarks; they are typifications, meta-commentaries, and more complex metaphorical comparisons, all of which might be thought of as schemas associated with particular domains of human behavioral practice.

Human Associated Schemas

"It's just like a little kid." "They look like old men."

"They're playing hide and seek." "They really are like people" "It's weird how they show affection just like humans" (1/18/2010)

…"Nice family reunion" [On observing grooming 9/5/09]

"They're cheerleaders … they got poms-poms" "They're playing peek-a-boo" (9/6/2009)

"He's [she's] in the Jacuzzi chillin' out." (1/18/2010)

"They're playin' at their house … They have a big house" (1/18/2010)

They're trying to decide what the next [football] play is" (Fieldnotes 1/17/10)

"Dad [Lorel] is just over there chillin' all by himself." (10/10/2009)

"They're in time out." (11/29/09)

There are several more MBAs that involve additional interpretive steps. These include (a) Self-comparison or comparison to a relative or friend, (b) Drawing moral lessons about the behavior being observed, and (c) Projecting intentionality onto the bonobos by speaking in the character of a bonobo actor. A few examples of each are given below:

Self-Comparison and Comparison to Kin or Friend

> "Yeah, it has a big boody. I have a big booty too." [elementary age child] (Fieldnotes 9/5/2009)

> "They're playing … same as you and your brother do." (Fieldnotes 1/17/10)

> "Looks like your uncle __ … see the big head" (9/6/10)

> Child "Monkeys are silly"… [Adult "dad"] – "Just like you. You're silly (9/6/10)

> "That looks like you ____" (1/18/2010)

> "Look he's doing tumblin' class just like you" [10/10/09]

Giving Voice

> "Thirsty time. I'm goin' to go get me a drink" [1/18/2010]

> "Come on. Give me the blanket … all right, I've got it" [1/18/2010]

> "Tag, you're it" (From YouTube posting "Silly Monkeys": daradg103. July 01, 2009

> I'm going to make you fall off!" [On bonobos playing on top of equipment 9/5/09, from "Bonobos at Jacksonville Zoo" http://www.youtube.com/watch?v=GdOlyY5DfJo]

> "I'm too sexy for my fur … I'm too sexy for my fur." [Fieldnotes 9/5/09]

Moralizing Lessons

"Hey, no biting" [Kid says, in observing tussle. 8/6/09]

"That one's cracked [the other] on the head … Don't do that." [1/17/10]

"Here they come … Let's see if they're going to be nice to each other again." [1/17/10]

"They were doing a naughty thing" [Mother to child on G-G rub, 9/5/09]

Finally we come to examples of the Misconceived Interpretive Schemas, where perception is influenced by strongly preformed cultural frames. I will talk here of three of these. As suggested above, one of the most prominent involves an assumption of maleness. This may reflect a broader pattern in our languaculture whereby the default sex for animals is male. (Zoo keepers and guides have told me that they often observe this to be the assumption of zoo visitors.) With bonobos, this misperception might also relate to people's lack of familiarity with their peculiar swellings and genital anatomy and to the older females being bald, due to over-grooming. Still, even the presence of the bonobo's swollen breasts can be missed, as in the case of the woman who said, "Look at that really hairy old guy that's holding it [the baby]," as she watched Kuni and her baby.

Another MIS involves the categorization error of lumping chimpanzee/bonobo/monkey into one group, with "monkey" as the prototypical exemplar. This lumping is most frequently expressed when people first arrive at the bonobo area and exclaim, "Look at the monkeys!" Upon leaving the area, parents also often tell their children, "Say 'bye-bye' monkey." And, while it is mostly children and adolescents who shout out "ooo-ooo aaah aaah" to the bonobos, adults occasionally may be observed doing this too, or an adult may encourage a child to "say 'oo-oo-oo'" (Fieldnotes 10/10/09). I have also observed children call out in this way at the squirrel monkey area and once, in another zoo, in front of orangutans.

Finally, a third MIS is what might be called the "Bonobo/Chimp as Silly Entertainer" frame of understanding. When the younger bonobos are active in playing, climbing, and chasing, one often hears "Silly monkey!" and this is when they draw the biggest crowds. When they are not being so entertaining, people might complain. On the one hand, you get comments like "He's so funny. Oh, silly monkeys!" ("More silly monkeys" [YouTube post: daradg103. July 01, 2009]) And "What do you think you're doing you crazy monkey!" [Fieldnotes 9/5/09]. On the other hand, you get whining comments such as "They're not very tricky. They don't do very much tricks" [Fieldnotes 1/1/10], "Wake up monkeys" [Fieldnotes 8/6/09], and "You all look dead" [Fieldnotes 9/6/09].

CONCLUDING COMMENT

One of the reasons I got involved in this study is that I thought it might help me in teaching. Firsthand observation of bonobos have helped me in this regard, but so has firsthand observation of other people watching them. The first thing I am going to try to employ in teaching is to activate the simplest features of the human-ape mirroring process by, for example, showing pictures and videos of bonobos and chimpanzees engaged in familiar activities. A first step in any social understanding is to have enough sympathy and/or empathy to be willing to step outside one's own shoes. It would be helpful, in this regard, to activate some of our fundamental thought processes that connect us to others, including animals. In this way, one might have a chance to reach out, even to those who have been taught to think primarily in terms of dominion over animals rather than in terms of shared connections with them.

More difficult, of course, is work required to overcome the stereotypes. What I am thinking at this point is that it may be more valuable to engage students in intensive observational exercises than to
simply point out to them the misconceptions evoked by preformed
frames.

ACKNOWLEDGMENTS

The author wishes to thank Jacksonville Zoo and Gardens for per-
mission to conduct this research and for the ready assistance of
the administration and zookeeping staff. He would particularly
like to thank Tracy Williams-Fenn, Great Apes Supervisor; Great
Ape Keepers, Sabrina Barnes and Nancy Kitchen; Delfi Messenger,
Director of Animal Programs; and Kelliann Whitney, Director of
Education.

NOTES

1. The amazing Lorel has since given birth to another. Her daughter,
Baker, was born April 19, 2011.

REFERENCES

Corbey, Raymond. 2005. *The Metaphysics of Apes: Negotiating the
    Animal-Human Boundary.* Cambridge: Cambridge
    University Press.

Fuentes, A., and Linda Wolfe, eds. 2002. *Primates Face to Face: The
    Conservation Implications of Human-Nonhuman Primate
    Interconnections.* Cambridge: Cambridge University Press.

Haraway, Donna. 1989. *Primate Visions: Gender, Race, and Nature in
    the World of Modern Science.* New York: Routledge,
    Chapman & Hall.

Iacoboni, Marco. 2008. *Mirroring People: The New Science of How We Connect with Others*. New York: Farrar, Strauss and Giroux.

Morris, Ramona, and Desmond Morris. 1966. *Men and Apes*. New York: McGraw Hill.

Ohnuki-Tierney, Emiko. 1987. *The Monkey as Mirror: Symbolic Transformations in Japanese History and Ritual*. Princeton: Princeton University Press.

Peterson, Dale, and Jane Goodall. 2000. *Visions of Caliban: On Chimpanzees and People*. Athens: University of Georgia Press.

Sponsel, Leslie. 1997. "The Human Niche in Amazonia: Explorations in Ethnoprimatology." In *New World Primates*, edited by W. Kinzey, 67-81. New York: Aldine de Gruyter.

Wheatley, Bruce P. 1999. *The Sacred Monkeys of Bali*. Prospect Heights, IL: Waveland.

The Kegare Concept

Lauren Levine

Kegare (穢れ) is a Japanese concept that refers to conditions of spiritual contamination, uncleanliness, or pollution. The concept is thought to have developed in the Yayoi period of prehistoric Japan. It was written about by the Chinese in the Han and Wei chronicle and was mentioned in the Japanese Kojiki in 712 (Norbeck 1952, 269). Like many concepts associated with religious ideals and behaviors in Japan, it combines Shintoistic properties with Buddhist ones. As anthropologist Joy Hendry (2003, 119) observes, "Most Japanese people can without conflict practice both Buddhist and Shinto rites, sometimes these are even combined." Because kegare is associated with menstruation, birth, death, and sickness, it can be frequently misunderstood as physical contamination. However, as my observations will show, the concern is not primarily over hygiene, but spiritual pollution.

The concept of pollution in Japanese society was more overt in previous eras and could even involve legal sanctions, but it has become more diluted over time. Laws originally in place regarding kegare have gradually been abolished. In 1872, for example, "the state abolished intragovernmental regulations regarding the birth *kegare*, a move that freed officials to go to work even if their wives or other female relatives had just given birth. Early in 1873 the council went a step further by abolishing any and all regulations designed to prevent the transmission of *kegare*" (Bernstein 2006, 62-64).

My experience suggests that today kegare has become more of a social ideology than a religious doctrine, and if asked what it involves and why, Japanese people cannot often give a clear explanation. Some of this lack of clarity stems from the fact that rituals or behaviors can be kegare in some situations, and acceptable in others. As I will show, this is because one of the most polluting acts that someone can commit is "mixing realms" or acting in a way that disrupts the "normal Japanese" life cycle pattern. Although in Japanese there are other terms that refer to pollution, such as *tsumi* (罪), often translated as sin, I have chosen to use *kegare* for all pollution terms, because it is the broadest.

During my nine-month stay as an exchange student in Nagoya, Japan, I encountered customs that emphasized compartmentalizing and putting boundaries around things for purposes of maintaining "cleanliness," even if there seemed to be little basis for this compartmentalization from the point of science—or even if the practices seemed contrary to a medical sense of hygiene. When we used exercise equipment at my host university, for example, it was expected that we would wipe down the machines with a dry washcloth. The stated reason for this was for the maintenance of hygiene, but this struck me as peculiar because no cleaning agent was used. It seemed to me that this was more of a ritual cleaning, rather than protection from bacteria. Another example supports this interpretation.

In the gymnasium, the kegare factor also regulated footwear. Unlike at many Japanese elementary and high schools, at my host university it was permissible to wear everyday shoes inside school. However, like most places in Japan, there are shoes that are designated only for gym areas, and you are not permitted to enter the gym wearing "outdoor shoes." Although called "outdoor shoes," the gym realm includes the tennis courts and the track. In the West, the distinction between gym shoes and street shoes is based on the type of shoe. The optimal shoe for places of exercise is one that supports the foot and does not harm the flooring or the gym equipment. The Western distinction is therefore about the type of shoe that should be allowed inside of a gym. In Japan, however, the stated reason is to maintain cleanliness. Yet, if students forget to bring their indoor shoes, it is permissible, at least in the case of my university, for them to enter the gym and use the equipment without shoes; they may either wear socks instead or just go barefoot. Since this seems particularly unhygienic, given the many people walking and running in these public areas and also dangerous on the exercise machines, there must be something else involved other than the cleanliness of shoes. It seems to me that this makes better sense in terms of kegare. The purpose of the shoes is to prevent the kegare of the outside world from entering the exercise area and to prevent the kegare of the exercise area from leaving.

Kegare can be seen again in the concept of bathroom shoes. In most family bathrooms, and in those of traditional Japanese hotels (*ryokans*), it is traditional to change out of one's shoes and into bathroom slippers. When the tradition of removing shoes before entering into any home is also taken into account, a clear pattern can be seen of compartmentalizing each area of life and using these compartments to prevent any kegare, or uncleanliness from a polluted realm, from spilling into areas of life where it does not belong.

That there are distinctly compartmentalized domains in Japan is by no means a new discovery. In her overview of Japanese culture, for example, Joy Hendry (2003, 44) points out that "*uchi* and *soto* are associated with the clean inside of the house, and the dirty outside world, respectively. Japanese houses almost always have an entrance hall where shoes, polluted with this outside dirt, are removed and it is one of the few inflexible rules enforced by Japanese adults that small children learn to change their shoes every time they go in and out of the house." *Uchi* (内) is the Japanese word for inside and *soto* (外) means outside. Hendry (2003, 46) goes on to say that uchi expands into different realms, and that "even for each of these 'inside' groups a slightly different type of behavior will be appropriate." There are other aspects of this that require elaboration. In my experience, there is not a set uchi, but a relative one. Depending on where someone was, or with what society they were currently associating, that became the uchi inside, and everything around them became soto. The only true soto that I found was that of being a *gaijin* (外人), a term used for foreigner but that literally means "outside person."

While the problem of mixing inside and outside things is evident enough from a Western perspective, it is also the case that mixing uchis produces kegare. Although many of the uchi's have slightly different types of appropriate behavior, some have behavior that committed anywhere else would be kegare. The perfect examples for this are prostitution and adultery. Until 1957, prostitution was still legal in Japan (Dore and Bendix 1967, 302). In historic Japan, it was normal for a section of the city to be designated for legal prostitution. But this has to be carefully regulated to maintain proper relations within the inside boundaries. This can be seen when all prostitution in Edo (today's Tokyo) was moved to the Yoshiwara district. "In the year 1617 ... the city in general was purified, and all the libertinism in it—permitted, but regulated—was banished to one special quarter" (Chamberlain 1971, 524). Currently, prostitution is illegal in Japan, but "massage" parlors and hostess bars that offer "private sessions" can still be found throughout the country. These places are not hidden in back alleys; they are clearly seen, and advertisements for them are freely distributed on the street. Women were, and some still are, expected to tolerate their husbands' visits to such places or their other infidelities. As long as the husband never mixed his adulterous life with his home life and continued to maintain his household appropriately, then he was not sanctioned.

Another category of kegare is *shi-e* (死穢). This is kegare that pertains to death, translating into English as "death impurity" (Abe 2001, 1). Death, the sick and dying, and corpses, are thought to be kegare, and great caution is taken around death to avoid its spread. In his dissertation on impurity and death in Japan, Abe (2001, 10) describes a scene from Medieval Japan that exemplifies this: "In 1107 a corpse was transported from the country of Owari (Nagoya) to the house of a samurai lord, Hyooenojoo Iesue in Kyoto. The lord's retainers, who were contaminated with shi-e of the corpse, walked around Kyoto and unwittingly polluted the whole city with *shi-e*. As a result, the government postponed sending imperial messengers to the highly sacred Ise shrine." Thus, the pollution from a corpse was thought to be able to spread, much like germs on one's hand.

I had a particular dramatic encounter with shi-e kegare in my experience in Japan when a fellow tenant of my apartment building committed suicide by jumping off the roof. A friend of mine discovered the still breathing man and called the police. The man died before he could be taken to a hospital, and once the body had been taken away, the focus of the police turned to disposing all evidence of the suicide, including the police tape, blood, and all police presence. The point was to make everything seem as if normal. The suicide occurred at around 3:00 a.m., but in less than two hours, by 5:00 a.m., there was no longer any sign of disturbance. Furthermore, there was no news coverage of the suicide, and the majority of the people in the building, including the owner, were not even aware of the incident. When my friend and I mentioned the death to people at our international center, we were expressly told not to mention it

again, even to our fellow exchange students. This was surprising to
me since an exchange student had found the body and because it is
common policy in the United States to provide a grief counselor to
students whenever an incident involving a traumatic death occurs.

Besides a corpse itself being kegare, an abnormal death can also
be polluting. As Lebra has noted, "Being killed or dying in a natural
disaster is as sinful, in the polluting sense, as killing" (1976, 238). In
an attempt to alleviate the problems associated with such an abnormal end to the course of a normal life cycle, the *hanayoume ningyou*
ritual (花嫁人形) was created. *Hanayoume ningyou* is Japanese for
"bride doll." This is a marriage ritual held for the spirit of a young
relative, such as a miscarried offspring or a victim of disease or war
who has died before being able to marry. The ritual is called "bride
doll" because if the partner is not thought of as another spirit, it is
said to be a doll. Typically a doll and a photo of the deceased are en-
cased in glass and kept so that offerings may be made regularly to it.
The doll's spirit is thought to care for and comfort the deceased as a
wife would a husband. Only after some thirty years of such comfort
is the deceased thought to feel satisfied enough to move on in the
spirit realm (Schattschneider 2001).

While death is one of the most polluting aspects of kegare, sickness, birth, and menstruation are also defiling. In *The Religions of
Japan from the Dawn of History to the Era of Meiji,* William Griffis
(2005, 85) observes that "Disease, wounds, and death were defiling,
and the feeling of disgust prevailed over that of either sympathy or
pity.... Anciently there were huts built both for the mother about to
give birth to a child, or for the man who was dying or sure to die of
disease or wounds. After the birth of the infant or the death of the
patient these houses were burned." With modifications, this is still
relevant.

In modern Japan, many medical situations are influenced by keg-are. For example, a patient's visit to a women's clinic is organized so that there is as little direct contact with her as possible. The patient covers her face at all times, and the doctor does the examination from a separate room. There is a half door that opens into the pa-tient's room so that there is an impression that the doctor is in a separate room even as a vaginal exam is done. Face-to-face meetings, even ones requested by the patient, are not allowed (Nadolny 2009). When past practices regarding women are taken into consideration, it appears to me that this practice is less about patient privacy and more about protecting the doctor from the kegare of the female body. In an important article written about post-war Japan called "Pollu-tion and Taboo in Contemporary Japan," Edward Norbeck (1952) wrote about how menstruating women took meals separately from other family members to avoid polluting them. The women would also carefully avoid any shrines and temples, and the hearth fire at the home had to be changed after the last day of her cycle. The *keg-are* of childbirth also lasted 32 days, and during this time the new mother could not leave the house through any of the rooms that held a household shrine. For the first 15 days, the mother must do no cooking, and if she went outside, she must cover her head in order to avoid defiling the sun (Norbeck 1952, 272-273). During the Heian period "women were considered creatures of deep sin, destined in death to be thrown into the pond of [their own menstrual] blood in hell" (Wakita 2006, 31). Today in Japan, menstruating females are allowed to enter shrines but are encouraged to enter by going around the shrine gate to avoid defiling the structure (Nishiwaki 2010).

The purity of food is of great importance to the Japanese. Histori-cally, so-called unclean people, called the *eta* (穢多) (the kanji can be translated to mean an abundance of kegare), were not allowed to grow rice or live near areas where rice was cultivated. Today great care goes into the packaging of foods into "pure" packages. An example is a package of cookies. Each cookie is wrapped separately in plastic, and then these cookies are placed into a plastic tray, and then this is wrapped in packaging identical to that found in the United States. In some bars that I have encountered, peanuts are placed in a bowl but are wrapped individually. This seems to contradict the stringent recycling laws that are found throughout Japan. While one could explain this packaging diligence as being there to avoid germs, food and drink is freely shared among friends, and in my experience there is no stigma between two friends, or even acquaintances, biting from the same sandwich or drinking from the same cup. Thus, it seems to make more sense as a manifestation of kegare.

Japan is a country that has traditionally had a rigid status system that some have likend to a caste system. It not only involved politics and economics but also regulated how one spoke. As Hendry notes, "Japanese language has quite clear speech levels, which are chosen according to the relationship between the people involved in a conversation, as well as the context in which they find themselves" (2006, 46).

At the bottom of the caste system were the eta people, now called *Burakumin*, who traditionally handled anything spiritually polluting. "The pariahs' main occupations were leather work, bamboo craft, itinerant entertainment, peddling, gardening and unskilled labor, such as animal slaughter and removing sewage. Work dealing with animals was considered not lowly but extremely defiling" (Shimahara 1948, 340). Although originally defined by job, the condition of being Burakumin was hereditary and was also thought to be able to spread by contact. Although the government outlawed the caste system after World War II, discrimination against the Burakumin continues. Discovering Burakumin heritage can stop an engagement, and the Burakumin people still live in mass in designated neighborhoods of old. In the family registries, although the term *eta* has been eliminated, the Burakumin people are now listed as "new people," making recognition simple (Haruna 2009). Traditionally these people were not allowed to interact with Japanese society, except in their designated unclean roles. "They were scavengers, buriers of the executed, skinners of animals and tanners of hides. They were Japan's untouchables, or more exactly, their uncountables, for even the mileage of roads through their villages went uncounted as if the land and the inhabitants of the area did not exist at all. They were desperately poor, and though guaranteed the exercise of their trades, they were outside the formal structure" (Benedict 1954 [1946], 61). Even the act of wearing a popular hairstyle was forbidden to the Burakumin during the Tokugawa period. This was to prevent the hairstyle from becoming kegare and pollution spreading to the wider Japanese population (Shimahara 1948, 341).

Before I left for my stay in Japan, I read the quintessential anthropological study on Japan, Ruth Benedict's book from the World War II era, *The Chrysanthemum and the Sword*. While surprised at the number of similarities between Benedict's Japan and the Japan I was seeing, I was interested that she never mentioned the term *kegare* in her work or talked about how pollution and cleanliness affected Japanese society. Her work focused on social patterns in Japanese society, especially those relating to honor, duty, and shame. Even the Burakumin people only received a brief mention in her book, far less than one page. Although not mentioned by name, I was able to find evidence of kegare in her book when Benedict talked about the soldiers who, when taken as prisoners of war, completely abandoned all ideas of returning to their family and focused on living their new lives in America. These people, by standards of Japanese definition, had become kegare. Instead of dying in battle, they had become "damaged goods" and had no hope of returning to their home country with honor. Even the wounded in battle were treated as damaged and were given little medical attention (Benedict 1954 [1946], 36-38). My explanation for the lack of mention of kegare and pollution in her book was that it was not described to her. Of course, when talking about Shinto rituals, cleanliness and pollution must be mentioned, but the far-reaching aspects of the related concepts themselves are rarely acknowledged. This might have had to do with the stigma associated with mentioning kegare. "Distancing itself from folk belief in *kegare* also contributed to the official effort to prove to the European and American powers, and to the emperor's subjects, that Japan was on track to becoming a modern, progressive nation devoted to 'civilization and enlightenment'" (Bernstein 2006, 65).

By way of conclusion, a brief discussion of the anthropology of purity and pollution is appropriate. In her classic analysis, Mary Douglas (2008 [1966], 489) found that there are four types of social pollution. "The first is danger pressing on external boundaries; the second, danger from transgressing the internal lines of the system; the third, danger in the margins of the lines. The fourth is danger from internal contradiction, when some of the basic postulates are denied by other basic postulates, so that at certain points the system seems to be at war with itself." In my time living in Japan, I found kegare to be a mix of the second and fourth definitions. Transgressing the internal lines of the system causes internal contradiction. Japanese society is so compartmentalized that the concepts of right and wrong are purely situational. When the standards of one uchi muddy the standards of another, kegare is born.

REFERENCES

Abe, Chikara. 2001. *Impurity and Death: A Japanese Perspective.* Ann Arbor: Accessed through dissertation.com.

Benedict, Ruth. 1954 [1946]. *The Chrysanthemum and the Sword.* North Clarendon: Tuttle.

Bernstein, Andrew. 2006. *Modern Passings: Death Rites, Politics, and Social Change in Imperial Japan.* Honolulu: University of Hawaii.

Chamberlain, Basil Hall. 1971. *Japanese Things; Being Notes on Various Subjects Connected with Japan, for the Use of Travelers and Others.* Rutland, VT: Tuttle.

Dore, Ronald Philip, and Reinhard Bendix. 1967. *Aspects of Social Change in Modern Japan.* Princeton: Princeton University Press.

Douglas, Mary. 2008 [1966]. "External Boundaries." In *Anthropological Theory: An Introductory History,* edited by R. Jon McGee and Richard L. Warms, 484-493. Boston: McGraw-Hill.

Griffis, William Elliot. 2005. *The Religions of Japan: From the Dawn of History to the Era of Meiji.* New York: Cosimo Classics.

Haruna, Nobuo. Spring 2009. Unpublished lecture notes. Japanese Culture Class. Nagoya: Chukyo University.

Hendry, Joy. 2003. *Understanding Japanese Society.* London: Routledge Curzon.

Lebra, Takie Sugiyama. 1976. *Japanese Patterns of Behavior.* Honolulu: University of Hawaii.

Nadolny, Erin P. Fall 2009. Personal communication. Shiogamaguchi, Japan: Chukyo University.

Nishiwaki, Emiko. Spring 2010. Personal communication. Cullowhee, USA: Western Carolina University.

Norbeck, Edward. 1952. "Pollution and Taboo in Contemporary Japan." *Southwestern Journal of Anthropology* 8(3):269-85.

Schattschneider, Ellen. 2001. "Buy Me a Bride: Death and Exchange in Northern Japanese Bride Doll Marriage." *American Ethnologist* 28(4):854-80.

Shimahara, Nobuo. 1948. "Toward the Equality of a Japanese Minority: The Case of Burakumin." *Comparative Education* 20(3):339-53.

Wakita, Haruko. 2006. *Women in Medieval Japan: Motherhood, Household Management and Sexuality*. Clayton: Monash Asia Institute.

Contributors*

CAITLIN AAMODT is an anthropology student at the University of Alabama at Birmingham who was awarded an NSF-REU Fellowship to Fiji in 2009 and 2010.

THOMAS BRASDEFER is a graduate student in Geography and Anthropology at Louisiana State University, minoring in linguistics. His work is mostly critical across the board of human sciences with a strong interest in subaltern cultures. He is currently writing his dissertation on the spatial and political aspects of indigenous language policy in the United States.

LORETTA A. CORMIER is an associate professor in the Anthropology Department at the University of Alabama at Birmingham. She is a cultural anthropologist with specializations in historical ecology, ethnoprimatology, and medical anthropology.

JADE DELISLE is a graduate student at the University of Alabama at Birmingham. In 2009-2010 Jade and Megan Noojin conducted laboratory analyses of archaeological remains from field sites in Nayau, Fiji.

SHARYN R. JONES is an assistant professor in anthropology at the University of Alabama at Birmingham specializing in ethnoarchaeology of the Pacific Islands.

LAUREN LEVINE is an undergraduate student of anthropology at Western Carolina University.

BRANDON D. LUNDY is an assistant professor in the Geography and Anthropology Department at Kennesaw State University in Georgia. His research is shaped by the practice of everyday life, conceptions of cultural identity, globalization, and political economy. At present, Dr. Lundy is working on an edited-volume on teaching Africa in the 21st century classroom and continues to collect ethnographic data on livelihood strategies in rural Guinea-Bissau, West Africa.

CHRISTOPHER MARINELLO is an applied anthropologist working as a US Peace Corps community health extensionist in the Dominican Republic. He is interested in community health issues and the anthropological analysis of the interface of knowledge and belief systems.

ANNA McCOWN is an anthropology student at the University of Alabama at Birmingham who was awarded an NSF-REU Fellowship to Fiji in 2009 and 2010.

MALLORY MESSERSMITH is an anthropology student at the University of Alabama at Birmingham who was awarded an NSF-REU Fellowship to Fiji in 2009 and 2010.

H. LYN WHITE MILES is UC Foundation Professor of Anthropology at the University of Tennessee at Chattanooga. Her research interests include the enculturation of Chantek and other great apes with sign language, tool-making, material culture, arts and crafts, games, problem-solving, navigation, and technology; orangutans; evolution of language and cognition, including theory of mind, imitation, self-awareness and empathy; great ape personhood; human cognitive, linguistic and symbolic evolution; and teaching of anthropology.

MEGAN NOOJIN is a graduate student at the University of Alabama at Birmingham. In 2009-2010, Megan and Jade Delisle conducted laboratory analyses of archaeological remains from field sites in Nayau, Fiji.

MILES RICHARDSON. The late Professor Richardson (1932-2011) wrote the following about himself: "Ever since receiving his doctorate from Tulane University in 1965, Miles found his place at Louisiana State University and in the Department of Geography and Anthropology. Before transferring to Tulane, he attended a year at LSU where the joint curricula open new vistas so going back permitted him to renew his contact with the vistas, allowed him to develop courses on the poetics of place and on human evolution, and to rant and rave in classes full of wonderful graduate students. His reading of George Hubert Mead, Berger and Luckmann, Ernest Becker, and above all, Miguel de Unamuno gave him the opportunity and courage to conceive culture as discourses about death." We reiterate here that this volume is dedicated to his life as a scholar, teacher, and humanitarian who represented the best ideals of anthropological holism.

MATTHEW RICHARD teaches and practices anthropology at Valdosta State University in Valdosta, GA. His interests include the mind and the brain, the political economy of the Toledo Maya, Czech and Roma social relations, and race and racism in the southern USA.

C. MATHEWS (MATT) SAMSON is visiting assistant professor of anthropology at Davidson College. His research interests include religious change and ethnic identity among the Maya in Guatemala, human rights concerns in Latin America, and human-environmental relations in Mesoamerica and in the US South and Southwest. His book *Re-enchanting the World: Maya Protestantism in the*

Guatemalan Highlands was published by the University of Alabama Press in 2007.

ROBERT SHANAFELT is an associate professor of anthropology at Georgia Southern University. Trained in four-fields of anthropology at the Kent State University and the University of Florida, he became more impassioned about the holism and synergy of anthropological perspectives after years of teaching in various areas of anthropology; all thanks to work in academic trenches known under the guise of the impoverished ecological niche known as "adjunct."

ANDREA ZVIKAS is a student at Valdosta State University.

---

*Note: This information reflects affiliations that were current in 2010 and does not reflect changes since then.

www.ingramcontent.com/pod-product-compliance
Lightning Source LLC
Chambersburg PA
CBHW020607270326
41927CB00005B/219